Ancient Paganism

The Sorcery of the Fallen Angels

by
Ken Johnson, Th.D.

Ancient Paganism
by Ken Johnson, Th.D.

Printed in the United States of America

ISBN 1439297703
EAN 9781439297704

Unless otherwise indicated, Bible quotations are taken
from the King James Version.

Table of Contents

Preface

The goal of this book is to define pre-flood paganism and its reoccurrence as the Mystery Religion established by Nimrod shortly after the Flood. We will do this by looking at some ancient history texts of the Jews and early church fathers.

We will define all the pagan practices and the sorcery of the pre-flood world, the ancient Canaanites, and medieval times and identify its existence today.

You will learn exactly how the ancient sorcerers did what they did, and why God calls what they did an abomination.

We can then find the remains of this sorcery in current pagan religions and folklore around the world today.

We will then examine how paganism spread into Christianity and how it will eventually become the Antichrist's religion.

The History of the Fallen Angels

The Fallen Angels

Angel Classes
The word used in the Bible for angel really means "messenger." Sometimes God sent a human messenger, like a prophet, to speak to someone. Most of the time in the Bible, the "messenger" is a non-human creature. God created these non-human messengers before humans and even before the planet earth was formed. Today, Christians refer to them as angels, although there are several types of "angels." Rabbinic legend tells us there are ten different types of angels. Biblically we know of at least four classes: cherubim, seraphim, angels, and archangels.

The Bible does not say exactly when or where the angels were created or how they exist. We do know that the angels were already in existence and Lucifer had already fallen when Adam was still in the Garden of Eden.

We know a lot about angels from Scripture. They are:

Spirit beings	Heb. 1:14
Created beings	Ps. 148:2,5
Invisible	2 Kings 6:15-17
Can materialize in human form	Gen. 18:2-8
Immortal	Luke 20:36
Holy	Matt. 25:31
Wise	2 Sam 14:17,20
Meek	Jude 9
Possess emotions	Luke 15:10
Innumerable	Heb. 12:22
Powerful	Ps. 103:20
Obedient to God	Ps. 103:20
Unmarried	Matt. 22:30
Do not create anything	John 1:1-3

Not perfect	Job 4:18
Concerned about human things	1 Pet. 1:12
Organized into orders or ranks	Isa. 6:2; 1 Thess. 4:16
Are a higher life form than man	Heb. 2:7
Worship Christ	Heb. 1:6
Know who are true Christians	Matt. 13:24-30,39
Will be judged by Christians	1 Cor. 6:3
Do not wish to be bowed down to	Rev. 19:7-10
Do not wish to be worshiped	Rev. 22:8-9
Can blind people	Gen. 19:10,11
Can mute people	Luke 1:20
Can kill	Isa. 37:36
Can cause plagues and death	Exod. 12:23
Can heal	John 5:4

They obviously have free will; or some of them would not have fallen. We also understand that since angels are a separate creation of God, men do not become angels after death.

Angels and Archangels

The Bible teaches angels and archangels look very much like men. The angel Gabriel looked so much like a human being that he is called a man sometimes in Scripture (Daniel 9:21). Gabriel revealed a prophecy to Daniel in 536 BC and announced the birth of Jesus to Mary about 2 BC.

Among the angels there are ranks. Some are referred to as princes and others as chief princes (Daniel 10:13). The exact meaning of these titles remains obscure.

Guardian Angels

The guardian angel is one who protects a Christian, or some special person God wants protected. We see many instances in Scripture where this occurs. Jesus mentions the little ones are protected by angels. In Acts 12, Peter's angel broke him out of jail; so the apostles were protected by them as well.

> "Take heed that ye despise not one of these little ones; for I say unto you, That in heaven their angels do always behold the face of my Father which is in heaven." *Matthew 18:10*

> "And they said unto her, Thou art mad. But she constantly affirmed that it was even so. Then said they, It is his angel. But Peter continued knocking: and when they had opened the door, and saw him, they were astonished." *Acts 12:15-16*

Death Angels

Angels are incredibly powerful beings. Most people today have no idea what an angel is really capable of. In the book of Isaiah there was an Assyrian army consisting of 185,000 seasoned warriors. They had besieged the city of Jerusalem; so God ordered an angel to intervene. In one night that *one* angel killed every single one of the 185,000 Assyrians!

> "Then the angel of the LORD went forth, and smote in the camp of the Assyrians a hundred and fourscore and five thousand: and when they arose early in the morning, behold, they were all dead corpses." *Isaiah 37:36*

Exodus 12:23 describes how an angel passed over the Egyptians and killed their firstborn during the tenth plague. This "destroyer" is mentioned again by Paul in 1 Corinthians 10:10. Paul is referring to the event recorded in Numbers 14:37, where the destroyer killed the ten spies who murmured about entering the Promised Land.

The Hebrew word used here is מגפה (magpah). It is an unusual word for plague. In the Bible we only see it here, in the death of the firstborn in Egypt, and in the plague that Phinehas stopped in Numbers 25:7,8. In other Jewish texts, the word is also used for the event where the angel slew the 185,000 Assyrians.

In Modern Hebrew the word מגפה (magpah) means a "stroke." So when an angel kills someone, it appears to be a stroke, brain hemorrhage, brain lesion, or an aneurism. This does not mean that everyone who has a stroke is killed by an angel.

Notice the parallels. The ten faithless spies wanted to give up the Promised Land; the Egyptians wanted to keep the Israelis from leaving Egypt and entering the Promised Land; and the Assyrians wanted to displace the Israelites out of their land. Each group was destroyed by angelic strokes. Remember that Ariel Sharon gave up the Gaza strip and within a year's time suffered a stroke!

Seraphim

The word *seraph* is a Hebrew word. When used as a noun it usually refers to fiery or poisonous serpents. As a verb it means "burning." Using the base word "seraph" leads us to believe that the seraphim are either aflame themselves or serpent-like or both.

Isaiah gave us a description of the seraphim angels. These fiery serpent-like seraphim are creatures with three pair (six) wings.

> "In the year that king Uzziah died I saw also the Lord sitting upon a throne, high and lifted up, and his train filled the temple. Above it stood the seraphims: each one had six wings; with twain he

> covered his face, and with twain he covered his feet, and with twain he did fly. And one cried unto another, and said, Holy, holy, holy, is the LORD of hosts: the whole earth is full of his glory." *Isaiah 6:1-3*

Cherubim

Today most of the cherub pictures and statues we see are made in the image of a baby human with little wings. This is not the biblical cherub.

The prophet Ezekiel had visions of cherubim in wheels and God's throne. Notice how he describes them from these two passages.

> "As for the likeness of their faces, they four had the face of a man, and the face of a lion, on the right side: and they four had the face of an ox on the left side; they four also had the face of an eagle." *Ezekiel 1:10*

> "And every one had four faces: the first face was the face of a cherub, and the second face was the face of a man, and the third the face of a lion, and the fourth the face of an eagle." *Ezekiel 10:14*

One can see the face of a cherub looks like the face of an ox, or a bull. This might be what the legend of the Minotaur is based on.

Ezekiel tells us that cherubim have four wings (two pair) with the basic form of a man, with the exception of cloven hoofs instead of feet. Their heads look much more like a bull's than a human's.

In Genesis we know cherubim were placed at the entrance to the Garden of Eden after the fall of man, to prevent Adam from re-entering the garden. This cherub had a special weapon.

> "So he drove out the man; and he placed at the east of the garden of Eden Cherubims, and a flaming sword which turned every way, to keep the way of the tree of life." *Genesis 3:24*

We also see decorative cherubim placed in the tabernacle around the mercy seat. Some scholars think these passages indicate cherubim are normally guardians of places and objects.

Where Did the Fallen Angels Come From?

Originally all the angels served and worshiped God, their creator. They were curious about the things God was creating and even curious about mankind. No angel is all-knowing. The holy angels still desire to figure out the prophecies given in the Scriptures of old.

> "Concerning this salvation, the prophets, who spoke of the grace that was to come to you, searched intently and with the greatest care, trying to find out the time and circumstances to which the Spirit of Christ in them was pointing when he predicted the sufferings of Christ and the glories that would follow. It was revealed to them that they were not serving themselves but you, when they spoke of the things that have now been told you by those who have preached the gospel to you by the Holy Spirit sent from heaven. Even angels long to look into these things." *1 Peter 1:10-12 NIV*

Ancient Paganism

When Lucifer rebelled, he deceived one-third of the angels into following him. He may have suggested God was not telling the truth about Himself and creation. We will study that in the chapter on Lucifer. Angels are sometimes referred to as "stars." This may mean they shine brightly, like stars.

> "And his tail drew the third part of the stars of heaven... And the great dragon was cast out, that old serpent, called the Devil, and Satan, which deceiveth the whole world: he was cast out into the earth, and his angels were cast out with him." *Revelation 12:4,9*

The Bible tells us that fallen angels differ from holy angels in that they:

Fell through pride	1 Tim. 3:6
Some are already imprisoned	2 Pet. 2:4; Jude 6
Hell is prepared for fallen angels	Matt. 25:41
Make war on the saints	Rev. 12:7-17

The ancient church fathers give us more confirmation about what has been discussed so far. They agree that Lucifer spoke though the serpent in the Garden of Eden, and that only fallen angels desire to be worshiped as gods.

> "This Eve, became the author of sin, when in the beginning, she was deceived by the serpent. That wicked demon, who also is called Satan, who then spoke to her through the serpent" *Theophilus 2.28*

> "...nor do the angels, inasmuch as they are immortal, either suffer or wish themselves to be called gods." *Lactanus 7:17*

Demons are either fallen angels or very closely associated with them. The Scriptures tell us that demons are:

Evil	Luke 7:21; 8:2
Powerful	Luke 8:29
Unclean	Matt. 10:1
Under Satan	Matt. 12:24-30
Possess humans	Matt. 8:28-29
Know their destiny	Matt. 8:28-29
Receive worship (sacrifices)	1 Cor. 10:20
Instigate error/heresy	1 Tim. 4:1

Scripture also teaches that demon possession:

Is not insanity	Matt. 4:24
Is not a disease	Mark 1:32

The Bible warns us not to accept the teaching of any angel that contradicts the teaching of Scripture (Galatians 1:8). Fallen angels can appear as holy angels and seem very convincing.

What did the fallen angels do and teach? To learn that, we must begin with Lucifer.

The Fallen Cherub

Lucifer

Lucifer's Description
What we know of Lucifer comes mainly from the Biblical books of Isaiah and Ezekiel. According to Ezekiel, Lucifer was an angel of the cherub class.

We learned in the first chapter that cherubs have the general form of a human, but their heads look more like a ox or bull with horns. They have cloven hooves instead of human feet and they have four wings (two pair of wings).

This description has led to the modern idea that the devil has horns and cloven hoofs and is completely red with a pointed tail.

Lucifer's Ancient History
Lucifer was the anointed cherub that covered the throne of God. He was created perfect; sinless like all the other angels. He was the highest of the angels, God's crowning achievement, but then iniquity was found in him.

> "…Thou sealest up the sum, full of wisdom, and perfect in beauty. Thou hast been in Eden the garden of God; every precious stone was thy covering, the sardius, topaz, and the diamond, the beryl, the onyx, and the jasper, the sapphire, the emerald, and the carbuncle, and gold: the workmanship of thy tabrets and of thy pipes was prepared in thee in the day that thou wast created. Thou art the anointed cherub that covereth; and I have set thee so: thou wast upon the holy mountain of God; thou hast walked up and down in the midst of the stones of fire. Thou wast

> perfect in thy ways from the day that thou wast
> created, till iniquity was found in thee."
> *Ezekiel 28:12-15*

The prophet Ezekiel tells us Lucifer was in the Garden of Eden. We know he was there when he tempted Eve. Ezekiel also wrote that Lucifer was completely covered with precious stones and he was a great musician. He lived and walked on fiery stones.

When the seventy disciples came back to Jesus, they told Him of their success and that even the demons were subject to them. Not only is Jesus all-powerful; but He is also all knowing. Jesus told them not to rejoice in the power He gave them but in the fact that they knew the truth. Jesus then told them that He actually witnessed the corruption and fall of Lucifer.

> "And he said unto them, I beheld Satan as lightning fall from heaven." *Luke 10:18*

Lucifer's Fall

What happened? How could a being created perfect suddenly, on his own, become corrupted and utterly sinful? In spite of all the riches and power he had, he wanted more. Ezekiel tells us he was corrupted by his own wisdom.

> "By the multitude of thy merchandise they have filled the midst of thee with violence, and thou hast sinned: therefore I will cast thee as profane out of the mountain of God: and I will destroy thee, O covering cherub, from the midst of the stones of fire. Thine heart was lifted up because of thy beauty, thou hast corrupted thy wisdom by reason of thy brightness: I will cast thee to the

ground, I will lay thee before kings, that they may behold thee." *Ezekiel 28:16-17*

Through his greed and pride he decided he wanted God's position. This thought must have driven him insane. He wanted to rule as God and be worshiped as God. Isaiah records the five "I will's" of Lucifer and the judgment God placed upon him.

"How art thou fallen from heaven, O Lucifer, son of the morning! how art thou cut down to the ground, which didst weaken the [preflood] nations! For thou hast said in thine heart, I will ascend into heaven, I will exalt my throne above the stars of God: I will sit also upon the mount of the congregation, in the sides of the north: I will ascend above the heights of the clouds; I will be like the most High. Yet thou shalt be brought down to hell, to the sides of the pit." *Isaiah 14:12-15*

Notice that Isaiah seems to indicate Lucifer will be brought down to the sides of the pit of hell because he tried to ascend to Godhood. Undoubtedly those who become convinced they are evolving into gods will suffer the same fate.

Many ancient church fathers teach the Isaiah 14 passage is referring to the fallen cherub, Lucifer. See *Origen OFP 1.5.5* for a detailed discussion of this.

Since Lucifer's fall, Scripture calls him Satan, which is Hebrew for "adversary." In Revelation, John writes that one third of the angels rebelled along with Lucifer and all were cast out of heaven.

Ancient Paganism

> "And his tail drew the third part of the stars of heaven... And the great dragon was cast out, that old serpent, called the Devil, and Satan, which deceiveth the whole world: he was cast out into the earth, and his angels were cast out with him."
> *Revelation 12:4,9*

Keep in mind that Lucifer was perfect and the wisest of the angels and still went insane. Isaiah and Ezekiel state he wanted to be worshiped as God. He literally wanted to replace God in heaven and sit on God's throne. Let's look closely at the Bible's teaching about God and then look at the above verses and see what went though Lucifer's mind.

God's Truth
The Bible clearly states there is only one God. The Old Testament prophets and the New Testament writers both acknowledge this fact.

> "Ye are my witnesses, saith the LORD... understand that I am he: before me there was no God formed, neither shall there be after me. I, even I, am the LORD; and beside me there is no saviour." *Isaiah 43:10-11*

> "Look unto me, and be ye saved, all the ends of the earth: for I am God, and there is none else."
> *Isaiah 45:22*

> "...some people actually worship many gods and many lords. But we know that there is only one God, the Father, who created everything, and we live for him. And there is only one Lord, Jesus Christ, through whom God made everything and through whom we have been given life."
> *1 Corinthians 8:5-6 NLT*

18

"Thou believest that there is one God; thou doest well: the devils also believe, and tremble. But wilt thou know, O vain man, that faith without works is dead?" *James 2:19-20*

Men are not now, nor will ever be, gods.

"Now the Egyptians are men, and not God; and their horses flesh, and not spirit." *Isaiah 31:3*

Colossians chapter one clearly shows that everything that exists was created by the one true God. And in Hosea God said:

"for I am God, and not man." *Hosea 11:9*

It was not "robbery" for Jesus to claim godhood because He is part of the Trinity. But it would be wrong for anyone or anything else to claim they are part of the godhead. See Philippians 2:6.

Putting these Scriptures together we understand that there is only one God. Angels and humans are not God in any way, shape, or form. This one true God has always been here and will always exist in His present form, with no change. There never has been any other god and there never will be any other god.

Lucifer's Lie

One might understand if Lucifer was angry with God, he might convince one third of the angels of heaven to leave heaven to be alone, away from God. But look at the verses given about Lucifer's fall. He wanted to be worshiped as God and actually tried to take God's throne. How could any rational being think for one second that he might have power enough to force the only creator God out of His throne? No rational being would. Nor would Lucifer; unless, he believed his own lie. What was Lucifer's lie?

Lucifer's lie was this: God is not separate from His creation. When God puts His spirit into a newly created being, He looses part of Himself. In the Jewish Kabala this concept is called the Doctrine of Emanations.

In other words, if God created 100 billion people and put His spirit into each one of them, at that point the Bible would say God is still 100% God and Man is 0% God. Lucifer, on the other hand, would say at that point God might be, say, 47% God and all humans collectively would equate to 53% God.

Lucifer might have actually believed that if there were enough angels they could overcome God and absorb the rest of what God once was. That, in effect, would kill off God. He probably believed this was the way it had been done for generations of gods/angels and universes.

The Doctrine of Emanations would become the basis of all future pagan religions on earth, and the primary cause of the earth's destruction by a world-wide flood.

The Fall of Adam
The biblical book of Genesis records that Adam and Eve, the first man and woman, were created perfect and sinless. They were placed in the Garden of Eden. Lucifer manipulated and then possessed a serpent and tempted Eve to sin. He knew that if he could get Adam and Eve to sin it would result in their death and destruction. God commanded them not to eat from the tree of knowledge of good and evil. Lucifer, through the serpent, deceived Eve by feeding her half truths mixed with doubt.

"...he said unto the woman, Yea, hath God said, Ye shall not eat of every tree of the garden? And the woman said unto the serpent, We may eat of the fruit of the trees of the garden: But of the fruit of the tree which is in the midst of the garden, God hath said, Ye shall not eat of it, neither shall ye touch it, lest ye die." *Genesis 3:1-3*

Once Lucifer got Eve to question exactly what God did say, he tempted her with the very thing that he was obsessed with: being God.

"And the serpent said unto the woman, Ye shall not surely die: For God doth know that in the day ye eat thereof, then your eyes shall be opened, and ye shall be as gods, knowing good and evil." *Genesis 3:4-5*

This was a half truth. Their eyes were opened in the sense they became aware of good and evil, but it also resulted in their physical and spiritual deaths. God expelled them from the Garden of Eden, but put into motion a plan of redemption. Centuries later Jesus would incarnate and live a sinless life and die on the cross to pay for the sins of Adam and Eve and all of us, their children.

The apostle Paul warned us not to believe the lies told by fallen angels.

"But though we, or an angel from heaven, preach any other gospel unto you than that which we have preached unto you, let him be accursed." *Galatians 1:8*

"Let no man beguile you of your reward in a voluntary humility and worshipping of angels, intruding into those things which he hath not seen, vainly puffed up by his fleshly mind," *Colossians 2:18*

"And no marvel; for Satan himself is transformed into an angel of light." *2 Corinthians 11:14*

Lucifer knew about God's plan for human redemption and put into motion his own plan to stop this from happening. His plan was to create a counterfeit religion to pull all the sons and daughters of Adam and Eve away from the true knowledge of God. And he did exactly that.

Enoch Hears From God

Pre-Flood History

The Bible tells us all life on earth was completely destroyed by a flood of water. Only Noah, with his wife, three sons and their wives, escaped on the ark with the animals to repopulate the planet.

What happened? How did the world become so corrupt that it had to be destroyed? It was Lucifer's lie!

Adam and Eve realized they had been deceived. They knew now they were not going to become gods. They rejected the lie and waited for God's promise of a redeemer. They had many children. Their third son was named Seth. Seth was born in the year 130 AM. "AM" stands for Anno Moundi, meaning "the year of the world." This would be the same as saying 130 years after creation. See *Ancient Post-Flood History* for more detailed descriptions of this history.

When Seth was 105 years old, he fathered a child named Enos. Enos was born in the year 235 AM. The ancient Jewish history book of Jasher, recommended reading by Scripture, states that at this time the first wave of apostasy started. See appendix A for information on this and other ancient history books and how to obtain them.

> "And Seth lived one hundred and five years, and he begat a son; and Seth called the name of his son Enosh, saying, Because in that time the sons of men began to multiply, and to afflict their souls and hearts by transgressing and rebelling against God. And it was in the days of Enosh that the sons of men continued to rebel and transgress against God, to increase the anger of the Lord against the sons of men." *Jasher 2:2-3*

"And the sons of men went and they served other gods, and they forgot the Lord who had created them in the earth: and in those days the sons of men made images of brass and iron, wood and stone, and they bowed down and served them. And every man made his god and they bowed down to them, and the sons of men forsook the Lord all the days of Enosh and his children;"
Jasher 2:4-5

When Enos was 90 years old he fathered a child he named Cainan. Cainan was wise and walked in the way of his great-grandfather Adam. Adam instructed Cainan about the Fall and the promised redemption and explained that God had revealed to him that the world would be destroyed once by water and once by fire. Adam knew these things were true but he did not know which destruction would occur first: the fire or the water.

Cainan learned that the flood of water would occur before the world's destruction by fire. Cainan began to preach repentance. After a few people began to repent and be converted, Adam decided that if he made Cainan reign as king in his place, Cainan might be able to start the revival Adam could not. So when Cainan was forty years old, in the year 365 AM, Adam made Cainan king. Cainan was successful in leading a small revival.

"And Cainan reigned over the whole earth, and he turned some of the sons of men to the service of God." *Jasher 2:14*

This revival lasted little more than forty years. Jasher records that during the lifetime of Cainan's son Mahalalleel, somewhere between 395 and 460 AM, the revival ceased and men began to rebel once again. This time the apostasy involved more people than before. Someone during this time invented an herb potion that caused miscarriages. From that time forward abortions were common place, and this angered God considerably.

> "For in those days the sons of men began to trespass against God, and to transgress the commandments which he had commanded to Adam, to be fruitful and multiply in the earth. And some of the sons of men caused their wives to drink a draught that would render them barren, in order that they might retain their figures and whereby their beautiful appearance might not fade." *Jasher 2:19-20*

The apostasy worsened as time went along. But in the year 622 AM, Enoch, the grandson of Mahalalleel, was born. When Enoch was 165 years old, he fathered a child that he named Methuselah. After Methuselah was born, Enoch began to grow closer to God and the teachings of our forefather Adam. In time, he began to convert a few people to follow the ways of God.

This was noticed by Cainan who was still ruling at the time. Cainan believed that Enoch was anointed by God in a very special way. Cainan chose to relinquish his throne and make Enoch king, in the year 687 AM.

Enoch lead the most powerful revival in the history of the pre-flood world. This revival lasted longer than any other. The 700's AM were marked with many turning to the service of the Lord. But this began to wane in the 800's AM.

A very strange thing began to occur among the believers. People who truly were worshipers of God fell into a trap set by Lucifer and the fallen angels.

The believers were influenced by the manners and customs of the pagans and unknowingly began to adopt the ideas and mannerisms of the pagans around them. They began to honor godly people more than they should. This created a type of idol within the true religion that abhors idols. The religious books and other objects became nothing more to them in time than holy relics. These things were simply misused.

As much as Enoch tried to counter this behavior, it was to no avail. More and more frequently, Enoch witnessed religious people venerating the relics. He could see, in their eyes, a kind of worship directed to him rather than to God. As a result, Enoch withdrew from public life.

He sequestered himself in his mountain home. His days were filled with the worship of God. He spent less and less time with people. This did not help the situation either. When this did not work he came back to his public life to teach and sternly warn them, but his warnings never really took hold.

So with Enoch's presence causing more harm than good, the Lord told Enoch that he would be taken away. Enoch then warned his son to try everything he could following his Rapture to turn the people's focus back to God and God alone.

In the year 897 AM, Enoch made his son, Methuselah, king and prepared to be Raptured. After the Rapture of Enoch, Methuselah held control over the kingdom but his power waned quickly. During all of this a great war was brewing.

The Hebrew historian, Josephus, gives us the history of the Sethite-Cainite Wars. Josephus reveals to us:

Adam's son Cain traveled far away from the land of Eden and founded a city, naming it after his firstborn son. In the course of time the descendants of Adam had spread out over the earth and there were several nations between the land of Nod and the land occupied by some of the descendants of Seth. Slowly the Cainite ways were adopted by all except the Sethites. Up until the Rapture of Enoch, the seventh generation from Adam, the Sethites lived in peace.

> "Now this posterity of Seth continued to esteem God as the Lord of the universe, and to have an entire regard to virtue, for seven generations; but in process of time they were perverted, and forsook the practices of their forefathers; and did neither pay those honors to God which were appointed them, nor had they any concern to do justice towards men. But for what degree of zeal they had formerly shown for virtue, they now showed by their actions a double degree of wickedness, whereby they made God to be their enemy." *Josephus 2.3.1*

How did this occur? When Enoch was no longer ruling on earth, the Cainites made their move. Josephus says Cain:

> "became a great leader of men into wicked courses. He also introduced a change in that way of simplicity wherein men lived before; and was the author of measures and weights. And whereas

they lived innocently and generously while they knew nothing of such arts, he changed the world into cunning craftiness. He first of all set boundaries about lands: he built a city, and fortified it with walls, and he compelled his family to come together to it; and called that city Enoch, after the name of his eldest son Enoch..."
Josephus 1.2.2

One of Cain's descendants was Tubal. Tubal was the first martial artist. The rabbis state he invented the perfect murder weapon, the sword. He followed in the ways of Cain and the fallen angels.

"But Tubal, one of his children by the other wife, exceeded all men in strength, and was very expert and famous in martial performances. He procured what tended to the pleasures of the body by that method; and first of all invented the art of making brass." *Josephus 1.2.2*

The Cainites waged war with the now complaisant Sethites, who thought they were following God, but were more obsessed with orders and relics.

"Nay, even while Adam was alive, it came to pass that the posterity of Cain became exceeding wicked, every one successively dying, one after another, more wicked than the former. They were intolerable in war, and vehement in robberies; and if any one were slow to murder people, yet was he bold in his profligate behavior, in acting unjustly, and doing injuries for gain." *Josephus 1.2.2*

Another trick of Satan is to get your eyes off God. Instead of trusting Him as your avenger, you seek your own justice, becoming very similar to those you seek to eliminate.

At this point the whole world grew totally apostate. Only Noah and his immediate family stood firm in their zeal for God.

> "But Noah was very uneasy at what they did; and being displeased at their conduct, persuaded them to change their dispositions and their acts for the better: but seeing they did not yield to him, but were slaves to their wicked pleasures, he was afraid they would kill him, together with his wife and children, and those they had married; so he departed out of that land." *Josephus 2.3.1*

We will see later that not even the sons of Noah were completely perfect before the Lord, but now we must ask these questions:

1. What was the religion of the fallen angels?
2. How did their religion cause the complete apostasy and destruction of the entire world?
3. Was Lucifer's lie part of the pre-flood paganism?

The Religion of the Fallen Angels

Ancient Pre-Flood Paganism

Lucifer's plan was to create varying kinds of paganism. Believers who refused to convert would be offered a form of paganism rising up from within the true religion. Paganism absorbed the majority of believers when they were lulled into a false religion that looked very much like the real thing they were used to. Next, a destructive war annihilated most of the few who still held to the truth. Finally, though a root of bitterness, the rest became just like the Cainites.

In chapter two we learned that Lucifer's lie was that the creator God was fading away and people and angels would become gods in His place. This lie became the basis for the pre-flood false religion and all the pagan religions after the Flood.

In the Beginning

In the book of Genesis we learn that God created the heavens and earth in seven days. As revealed throughout the Bible, God is a personal, intelligent, loving Being that wishes to have a personal relationship with each human being.

When Adam fell, he took on a sin nature. All his children inherited this sin nature. Eventually all humanity, except Noah and his family, degenerated into apostasy. They rejected the knowledge and worship of the one true God, turning to idols and what would later be called paganism.

The following quotes from the Bible, early church fathers, and the ancient history books of the Jews, give us a glimpse of what pre-flood paganism actually was. From these we can put together thirteen points that paint a clear picture of what the great lie consisted of and how it destroyed the ancient world.

The apostle Paul wrote that the pre-flood world knew God's truth. They understood that God was completely separate from His creation. They also knew His power and Godhead were eternal, that there would never be any other gods. All of nature showed them that Lucifer's Doctrine of Emanations was a lie. They deliberately rejected the true knowledge of God and willingly accepted Lucifer's lie. They began to believe that their ancestors were evolving into gods and they began making idols.

> "For the invisible things of him from the creation of the world are clearly seen, being understood by the things that are made, even his eternal power and Godhead; so that they are without excuse: Because that, when they knew God, they glorified him not as God, neither were thankful; but became vain in their imaginations, and their foolish heart was darkened. Professing themselves to be wise, they became fools, And changed the glory of the uncorruptible God into an image made like to corruptible man, and to birds, and to fourfooted beasts, and creeping things."
> *Romans 1:20-23 KJV*

1. Individual Idols

The first point is each person made his own individual idol for his own home. Having idols proves they were not atheists. We will see that each idol was different because each person was worshiping his own ancestor. If they worshiped their ancestors, they must have believed their ancestors, and eventually they too, would evolve into gods. See Teraphim in the chapter on Babylon.

Ancient Paganism

> "And the sons of men went and they served other gods, and they forgot the Lord who had created them in the earth: and in those days the sons of men made images of brass and iron, wood and stone, and they bowed down and served them. And every man made his god and they bowed down to them, and the sons of men forsook the Lord all the days of Enosh and his children;"
> *Jasher 2:4-5*

Eve

The Sumerians, thought by many Christians to be representatives of the pre-flood world, worshiped a goddess they referred to as Nin.ti. Nin.ti is usually translated the "Lady of Life," but the literal translation is the "Lady of the Rib." See *Dictionary Of Deities And Demons In The Bible,* page 316. This is just one more example of pre-flood peoples worshiping their ancestors, including Adam and Eve.

2. Evolve into a god

Satan tempted Eve by saying she could become just like God. In pre-flood paganism, Satan told people they could become gods themselves. First century magicians thought after death they would become daemons, or helper spirits like elves or angels. But we learn though church father Tertullian, in the original pre-flood idolatry, people believed after death they were supposed to become a god.

> "In this way, even by magic, which is indeed only a second idolatry, wherein they pretend that after death they become demons, just as they were supposed in the first and literal idolatry to become gods." *Tertullian Treatise on the soul 57*

"God knows that your eyes will be opened when you eat it. You will become just like God, knowing everything, both good and evil."
Genesis 3:5 NLT

3. The original Creator God no longer exists

The third point of their pagan religion is that they taught the original Creator God no longer exists. The original creative force/god emptied itself into creation and no longer existed. We learned in chapter two, this was Lucifer's original lie.

"And they called to Noah, saying, Open for us that we may come to thee in the ark – and wherefore shall we die? And Noah, with a loud voice, answered them from the ark, saying, Have you not all rebelled against the Lord, and said that he does not exist?" *Jasher 6:18-19*

Again, these people were idolaters, not atheists. They believed that the original God ceased to exist or at least was greatly diminished and would soon disappear for all eternity.

4. Salvation is not needed.

The fourth point is there was no need for salvation. Any kind of salvation would be done "by their own strength." All will make it to godhood on their own, eventually. Magic just speeds up the process. This also included the idea that there is no hell (See the chapter on Paganism in the Middle Ages for details on hell).

"The LORD saw how great man's wickedness on the earth had become, and that every inclination of the thoughts of his heart was only evil all the time." *Genesis 6:5 NIV*

"They were despisers of all that was good, on account of the confidence they had in their own strength." *Josephus Ant. 1.3.1*

5. Observed omens in the sun and moon and
6. Charted their movement through the Zodiac.

The fifth and sixth points are that they used a form of astrology that centered on predicting omens, like eclipses, in the sun and moon and charted their courses through the zodiac. This was practiced as a means to summon the magic energies for rituals and to contact their ancestor gods at the appropriate times.

"And Cainan grew, and his father taught him writing, and he went to seek for himself a place where he might seize for himself a city. And he found a writing which former generations had carved on the rock, and he read what was thereon, and he transcribed it and sinned owing to it; for it contained the teaching of the Watchers in accordance with which they used to observe the omens of the sun and moon and stars in all the signs of heaven. And he wrote it down and said nothing regarding it; for he was afraid to speak to Noah about it lest he should be angry with him on account of it." *Jubilees 8:1-5*

7. No horoscopes

The pre-flood astrology did not have the idea of a horoscope. The horoscope was invented after the Flood by the Chaldeans. In the pre-flood version astrology was only used to predict the next scheduled date for magic rites and the next time one could contact a god or goddess ancestor.

"The Horoscope was invented by the Chaldean astrologers." *Hippolytus Heresies 4.3*

8. Invented by demons

The pre-flood magic system, including astrology, was the invention of demons.

"Demons invented the concept of fate with astrology to enslave man into worshiping them."
Tatian to the Greeks 9

9. Ritual use of Blood

Blood sacrifices, magic, demonology and ritual drinking of blood was used by post-flood Canaanites. The ritual use of blood was also part of the pre-flood religion. All animal sacrifices involved blood, but they are always referred to as animal sacrifices. When a ritual called for a blood sacrifice instead of an animal sacrifice we know it means the use of blood. The blood is what was needed, not necessarily the sacrifice of a living animal.

"In the twelfth generation, when God had blessed men, and they had begun to multiply, they received a commandment that they should not taste blood, for on account of this also the deluge had been sent... In the fourteenth generation one of the cursed progeny (Canaanites) first erected an altar to demons, for the purpose of magical arts, and offered there blood sacrifices."
Recognitions of Clement 1.30

God knew this false religion would return after the Flood; so He commanded Noah to ensure his children would not consume blood when eating meat.

"Every moving thing that is alive shall be food for you; I give all to you, as I gave the green plant. Only you shall not eat flesh with its life, that is, its blood." *Genesis 9:3-4 NASB*

10. Evolution / Reincarnation

All pagan religions teach reincarnation with evolution. A pagan religion can't have one without the other. Likewise the religions of the Christians and Jews teach special creation along with resurrection. These two can't be divorced, either. If we can prove evolution will be a part of the harlot church, we then know reincarnation will be, too. The book of Revelation shows the end time church becomes part of the Mystery Babylon religious system. Second Peter's prophesy states that it begins by the church rejecting creation and Noah's Flood, in favor of Evolution. This is taking place today in many denominations.

"there shall come in the last days scoffers, walking after their own lusts, And saying, Where is the promise of his coming? for since the fathers fell asleep, all things continue as they were from the beginning of the creation. For this they willingly are ignorant of, that by the word of God the heavens were of old, and the earth standing out of the water and in the water: Whereby the world that then was, being overflowed with water, perished."
2 Peter 3:3-6

"I saw a woman sitting on a scarlet beast... This title was written on her forehead: "Mystery Babylon the great, mother of prostitutes and of the abominations of the earth."
Revelation 17:3,5 NIV

11. Evolution without karma

The belief that each person was evolving into a higher life form was part of the pre-flood religion. Post-flood paganism added the doctrine of "transmigration of souls," which means if your "karma" or life style is very bad, instead of evolving into a *higher* life form, one may "de-evolve" or come back as a *lower* form of life. The doctrine of "karma" was not part of the original paganism. This makes sense, because Lucifer wanted everyone to believe there is no hell and we are all okay, so you can only go forward. We will see this again in the post-flood histories.

> "But I cannot here omit that which some erring philosophers say, that men and the other animals arose from the earth without any author."
> *Lactantius Divine Institutes 2.11*

> "Plato, that ancient Athenian, who also was the first to introduce this opinion (the doctrine of transmigration of souls)."
> *Irenaeus Against Heresies 2.33*

12. Ghosts, Demons, and Nature Spirits

Nature spirits were thought to be the life force in all of creation. This is connected to pantheism. If at death our spirits could evolve into a god, then the worship of demons and ghosts would be prominent. Notice their idols were not just demons and nature spirits, but also phantoms. "Phantom" is the Greek word for ghost.

> "You who serve stones, and ye who make images of gold, and silver, and wood, and stones and clay, and serve phantoms, and demons, and spirits"
> *Tertullian Idolatry 1.4*

13. Homosexual Marriage

There has always been homosexuality. It has always been classified as a sin before God. The Canaanites practiced homosexual rituals in the worship of their gods and goddesses, but since the time of Noah there has never been a nation that sanctioned homosexual marriage. But the rabbis state this did occur right before Noah's Flood. This may have been a part of the pre-flood religion; or it just may have been a result of it.

In Romans 1, the apostle Paul seems to indicate that idolatry produced immorality; and together idolatry and immorality caused the Great Apostasy. That, in turn, resulted in extreme forms of homosexuality, which caused God to destroy the world.

"Professing themselves to be wise, they became fools, And changed the glory of the uncorruptible God into an image made like to corruptible man, and to birds, and fourfooted beasts, and creeping things. Wherefore God also gave them up to uncleanness through the lusts of their own hearts, to dishonour their own bodies between themselves: Who changed the truth of God into a lie, and worshipped and served the creature more than the Creator, who is blessed for ever. Amen. For this cause God gave them up unto vile affections: for even their women did change the natural use into that which is against nature: And likewise also the men, leaving the natural use of the woman, burned in their lust one toward another; men with men working that which is unseemly, and receiving in themselves that recompence of their error which was meet. And even as they did not like to retain God in their knowledge, God gave them over to a reprobate mind, to do those things which are not convenient." *Romans 1:22-28*

The ancient rabbis seem to believe this also. They stated the practice of ordaining homosexual marriage was the last step in the downward spiral that caused God's judgment.

"Rabbi Huna said in the name of Rabbi Joseph, 'The generation of the Flood was not wiped out until they wrote marriage documents for the union of a man to a male or to an animal.'" *Genesis Rabbah 26:4-5; Leviticus Rabbah 23:9*

"Rabbi Hiyyah taught: The passage reads 'I am the Lord, your God' two times – I am the One Who punished the generation of the Flood, and the people of Sodom and Gomorrah, and Egypt; and in the future I will punish those who do as they did. The generations of the Flood were kings, and were wiped off the earth when they were soaked in sexual sin." *Leviticus Rabbah 23:9 (commentary on Leviticus 18:3)*

"And what did they do? A man got married to a man, and a woman to a woman, a man married a woman and her daughter, and a woman was married to two (men). Therefore it is said, "And you shall not walk in their statutes" *Sifra Acharei Mot, Parashah 9:8 (Commentary on Leviticus 18:3)*

Church fathers Clement of Alexandria (ECF 2.77) and Tatian (ECF 2.143) tell us that the ancient Romans and barbarians considered homosexuality and pederasty crimes punishable by death. In the first century, however, homosexuality and pederasty were widely practiced by the Romans.

When all this came about and Noah and his family were the only ones left still faithful to God, God instructed Noah to build the Ark and the world was then destroyed by a flood of water.

> "And God looked upon the earth, and, behold, it was corrupt; for all flesh had corrupted his way upon the earth. And God said unto Noah, The end of all flesh is come before me; for the earth is filled with violence through them; and, behold, I will destroy them with the earth." *Genesis 6:12-13*

Conclusion

These points give the following picture for pre-flood paganism:

The original creator/force emptied itself into creation. The spirit/life exists in everything (this is called pantheism). There is no need for salvation because everyone will eventually evolve into a god. Contacting your ancestors who have already ascended, and using magic, are short cuts to obtaining godhood. Using astrology to calculate the proper times for magic rites and speaking to your dead ancestors speeds up the process of godhood evolution.

One can't "de-evolve" (compared to Hinduism's doctrine of karma). Contacting the nature spirits may also help in your evolution. The magic rites included blood rituals.

On the following page is a master chart compiling all the above data from the source material. In a later chapter we will examine the Canaanite occultic practices individually and add them to the master chart.

Pre-Flood paganism included:
1. A unique individual god/idol in each home
2. Evolution into a god or goddess after death
3. The original creator God ceased to exist
4. Salvation not needed
5. Observation of the sun and moon for omens
6. Astrology focusing on the sun, moon, and zodiac
7. Astrology without horoscopes
8. Invented by demons
9. Ritual use of blood
10. Evolution/Reincarnation
11. Evolution without karma (no de-evolving)
12. Ghosts, demons, nature spirits
13. Homosexual marriage

After Noah's Flood

Eight Post-Flood Pagan Holy Days

The Four Holidays

According to chapter six of the Book of Jubilees, Noah decreed that four holidays be commemorated. These commemorated the new moons of the first, fourth, seventh, and tenth months. These were the turn of the seasons. Unlike the Noahide laws which were given by God to us through Noah, these were an invention of Noah himself; therefore we need not observe them.

"On the new moon of the first month, the new moon of the fourth month, the new moon of the seventh month, and the new moon of the tenth month are the days of remembrance, and the days of the seasons in the four divisions of the year. These are written and ordained as a testimony for ever. And Noah ordained them for himself as feasts for the generations forever, so that they have become thereby a memorial unto him. And on the new moon of the first month he was bidden to make for himself an ark, and on that day the earth became dry and he opened the ark and saw the earth. And on the new moon of the fourth month the mouths of the depths of the abyss beneath were closed. And on the new moon of the seventh month all the mouths of the abysses of the earth were opened, and the waters began to descend into them. And on the new moon of the tenth month the tops of the mountains were seen and Noah was glad. And on this account he ordained them for himself as feasts for a memorial forever, and thus are they ordained."
Jubilees 6:23-28

Ancient Paganism

Notice Jubilees has the events of the fourth and tenth months correct but event of the seventh month is incorrect according to the Bible. The command to build the ark was probably in the seventh month, not the first, because we learn from the Talmud that the new moon of the first month, Tishrei, is the anniversary of Creation and also when Noah was born. I believe it is more likely that the events were assigned to these dates by Noah's children rather than by Noah, himself. This commemoration will be twisted into ancestor worship later. Jubilees also states Noah commanded his children to observe the anniversary of the flood. This occurred on the seventeenth day of the second month, or two days after the lunar reckoning of the autumn equinox. Paganism calls this day Samhain, but today it is known by the name Halloween.

New Moon	Season	Event Commemorated
first month	Autumn	Creation and Noah's birthday
fourth month	Winter	Abysses were closed
seventh month	Spring	Commanded to build the Ark
tenth month	Summer	Tops of the mountains were seen

Full Moon	Season	Event Commemorated
second month	Autumn	Noah's Flood

Whether or not this legend is entirely true, it is obvious that early peoples had to commemorate the change of the seasons in order to keep crops planted at the right times and to be able to hunt animals for food without completely destroying their food supply. There are exactly thirteen weeks for each of the four seasons in a fifty-two-week year. In time, the mid-seasonal festivals were added, creating eight holy days per year.

As paganism developed, these events and the history about the evilness of pre-flood mankind and Noah's Flood would be twisted by Satan.

A lunar calendar month always starts on a new moon. Festivals usually fall on the fifteenth (the full moon) of the month.

As we go from the lunar calendar used by most of the ancient world (Jews, Babylonians, Canaanites, and most pagan groups today), to a solar calendar used by the ancient Romans and most of the world today, including America and Europe, these dates will vary slightly depending on the group or religion using them.

Here is a comparison between the ancient lunar calendar and the American calendar.

Lunar Calendar		Solar Calendar
New moon of the 1st month	Autumn equinox	Sept 21
Full moon of the 2nd month	Mid-autumn	October 31
New moon of the 4th month	Winter solstice	Dec 21
Full moon of the 5th month	Mid-winter	February 2
New moon of the 7th month	Spring equinox	Mar 21
Full moon of the 8th month	Mid-spring	May 1
New moon of the 10th month	Summer solstice	June 21
Full moon of the 11th month	Mid-summer	July 31

The following shows the four dates for the change in seasons and the Gentile names given to each one.

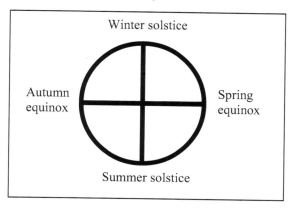

Season Change	Date	Gentile Names
Autumn equinox	Sept 21	Mabon
Winter solstice	Dec 21	Yule, Saturnalia
Spring equinox	Mar 21	Oestara
Summer solstice	June 21	Litha

When we add the four Mid-seasonal holidays to the above four holidays that begin the seasons, we have a total of eight holy days.

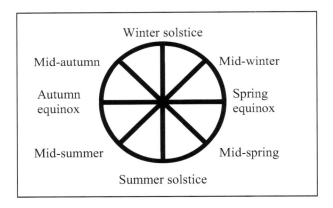

Mid Season	Date	Gentile Names
Mid-Autumn	October 31	Halloween, Samhain
Mid-Winter	February 2	Ground Hog Day, Candlemas, Imbolc, Oimelc, Brigid
Mid-Spring	May 1	May Day, Beltaine, Walpurgis Night
Mid-Summer	July 31	Lunasa, Lammas

We are not sure about the set times of the pre-flood pagan system, since they may not have had seasons like we do today. But with Nimrod's revival of the system, these eight days will be the basis for all pagan holidays.

Accurately predicting these eight days plus the solar and lunar eclipses for magic rituals was to be the primary use of astrology until the Chaldeans invented the horoscope.

We can see that the four main pagan holidays were practiced by Sodom. Homosexuality and extreme paganism is what caused God to obliterate the city.

> "In those days all the people of Sodom and Gomorrah, and of the whole five cities, were exceedingly wicked and sinful against the Lord... And they had in their land a very extensive valley, about half a day's walk, and in it were fountains of water and a great deal of herbage surrounding the water. And all the people of Sodom and Gomorrah went there *four times in the year*, [author's emphasis] and with their wives and children and all belonging to them, and they rejoiced with timbrels and dances. etc." *Jasher 18:11-13*

The Post-Flood Outbreak

Both the ancient rabbis and church fathers taught that Egypt was the first to bring back the magic system of the pre-flood world. This started to spread into

Mizraim	Egypt
Nimrod	Babylon
Canaan	Canaan
Sodom	Sodom

various countries though the sons of Ham, according to the Jewish history book of Jubilees. This occurred after Canaan started settling the coast of Canaan/Israel.

> "And Cainan grew, and his father taught him writing, and he went to seek for himself a place where he might seize for himself a city. And he found a writing which former generations had carved on the rock, and he read what was thereon, and he transcribed it and sinned owing to it; for it

49

contained the teaching of the Watchers in accordance with which they used to observe the omens of the sun and moon and stars in all the signs of heaven. And he wrote it down and said nothing regarding it; for he was afraid to speak to Noah about it lest he should be angry with him on account of it." *Jubilees 8:1-5*

The ancient church fathers wrote that Ham was the first post-flood magician. He must have revived these pre-flood practices and handed them down to his sons. The quote above makes it seem like finding and translating the pagan relics was the basic cause of the revival of the old religion. Lucifer's lie once again caused them to doubt Noah's history, even though he was an eye witness of the destruction. We need to be aware of what we read and watch on TV. It could influence us in ways we don't realize.

Egypt
Ham's son Mizraim founded Egypt. The Bible records how the Egyptian magicians withstood Moses. So even 792 years after the Flood, the old system was still going strong. We will see what Egyptian magicians do when we study Balaam.

Canaan
Ham's son Canaan traveled up the cost of Shem's territory and founded the Canaanites. The ancient rabbis give us detailed information about how the Canaanite sorcerers practiced their religion.

Persians and Babylonians
The Persians were descendants of Elam, the son of Shem, but the Persian magi inherited their magic system from the time Nimrod ruled over them. Nimrod was the

grandson of Ham. Nimrod invaded Iraq and founded the first Babylonian empire.

Sodom

The city of Zoar was founded by Bela. Bela was an Assyrian who left Assyria and came to Caanan, which is in the territory Noah gave to Shem, his forefather, and founded his town there. So he had every right to settle there. Bela left his homeland because of Nimrod's evil government. The city of Zoar stayed away from paganism. The cities of Sodom and Gomorrah were founded by Canaanites and in time they adopted paganism to such an extreme measure God destroyed them with fire. This is why Lot went to Zoar and the city of Zoar was spared.

In order to understand the outbreak of ancient paganism, we need to look at the religious / magic systems of Egypt, Babylon, Canaan, and Sodom.

We will first look at Nimrod's religion and the practices of ancient Sodom.

The Dead Sea

(Under this sea of salt the ruins of Sodom lie)

Babylon and Sodom and Gomorrah

Post-Flood Babylon

We know what the pre-flood pagan system consisted of from the chapter on pre-flood history. Let's look at what Nimrod added to the mix.

Nimrod added the idea that the twelve signs of the zodiac were gods in their own right. So he did not just worship his ancestors, but natural spirits (or nature spirits) as well. We will see how the concept of nature spirits develops though the Middle Ages in a later chapter.

> "And Abram asked his father, saying, Father, tell me where is God who created heaven and earth, and all the sons of men upon earth, and who created thee and me. And Terah answered his son Abram and said, Behold those who created us are all with us in the house. And Abram said to his father, My lord, shew them to me I pray thee; and Terah brought Abram into the chamber of the inner court, and Abram saw, and behold the whole room was full of gods of wood and stone, twelve great images and others less than they without number." *Jasher 11:19-20*

Ancient church father Clement of Rome stated the religion of the fallen angels included magic and incantations and this pre-flood religion was the basis for the post-flood Egyptian, Canaanite, Persian, and Babylonian magic systems. This led to diverse and erratic superstitions among the divisions of the post-flood nations.

> "Fallen angels taught men the use of magical incantations that would force demons to obey

them. After the flood Ham the son of Noah unhappily discovered this and taught it to his sons. This became ingrained into the Egyptians, Persians, and Babylonians. Nimrod was handed this knowledge and by it caused men to go away from the worship of God and go into diverse and erratic superstitions and they began to be governed by the signs in the stars and motions of the planets." *Recognitions of Clement 4.26-29*

The twelve zodiac gods and numerous other ancestor gods were worshiped in ancient Babylon. The Babylonian God, Marduk, was based on Nimrod's son, Mardon. See *Ancient Post-Flood History* for details.

Post-Flood Sodom

The book of Jasher provides over five pages of detailed information about the social structure, form of government, and extreme fornication and homosexuality of Sodom. In addition to these descriptions, Jasher recorded their religious practices. Sodom was the first recorded city that observed the four pagan holidays we just learned about in the previous chapter. Occultic rituals were held at waterfalls near forests and included sex, dances, and percussion instruments for a beat.

"And they had in their land a very extensive valley, about half a day's walk, and in it there were fountains of water and a great deal of herbage surrounding the water. And all the people of Sodom and Gomorrah went there four times a year, with their wives and children and all belonging to them, and they rejoiced there with tambourines and dances. And in the time of rejoicing they would all rise and lay hold of their neighbor's wives, and some, the virgin daughters of their neighbors, and they enjoyed them, and each man saw his wife and daughter in the hands of his neighbor and did not say a word. And they did so from morning to night, and they afterward returned home each man to his house; so they always did four times in the year." *Jasher 18:12-15*

Teraphim
The teraphim were idols used in ancestor worship. They were supposed to allow you to communicate with your ancestors at the proper astrological times. My guess is that the teraphim were not a new invention, but a continuation from the pre-flood world.

There are two types of teraphim mentioned in the book of Jasher. The first type was created by taking the first born male of the family and cutting off his head. The victim's head was supposed to retain contact with the departed spirit. With the proper ritual, the mummified head could serve as a conduit to the spirit world, passing information between a family and their ancestor gods.

The second type of teraphim was created by constructing an idol of the deceased and was used in the same way. The rituals had to be done at the proper astrological time. The ceremony used candles and other paraphernalia. Laban's teraphim were the second type: little gold gods with the astrological tables carved on them, rather than the first type mentioned, the mummified head of a real ancestor.

"And this is the manner of the images; in taking a man who is the first born and slaying him and taking the hair off his head, and taking salt and salting the head and anointing it in oil, then taking a small tablet of copper or a tablet of gold and writing the name upon it, and placing the tablet under his tongue, and taking the head with the tablet under the tongue and putting it in the house, and lighting up lights before it and bowing down to it. And at the time when they bow down to it, it speaketh to them in all matters that they ask of it, through the power of the name which is written in it. And some make them in the figures of men, of gold and silver, and go to them in times known to them, and the figures receive the influence of the stars, and tell them future things, and in this manner were the images which Rachel stole from her father, Laban." *Jasher 31:41-43*

In ancient Egypt, Canaan, and other places, archeologists have found communities with bones of infants buried in the walls of most homes. We can see this is connected to the teraphim form of ancestor worship.

The ancient pagans believed that contacting the nature spirits helped in their evolution. The magic rites included blood rituals, burning candles, astrology, and idols/teraphim.

The Egyptians had burial grounds for regular Egyptians (Jasher 14:13-14); but they buried their firstborn children in the walls of their homes. This was the Egyptian form of teraphim. Jasher records that when the death angel killed all the first born in Egypt, the angel also tore the remains of the sacrificed firstborn children out of the walls of the Egyptian houses (Jasher 80:44-46).

This information indicates the plague of the firstborn was directed against the teraphim, showing that the God of Israel was superior to all the so-called gods of Egypt, including all their ancestor gods!

If we add this information to our master chart of the pre-flood pagan religion, we have the following:

Pre-Flood paganism includes
1. An unique individual god/idol in each home
2. Evolution into a god or goddess after death
3. The original creator God ceased to exist
4. Salvation not needed
5. Observation of the sun and moon for omens
6. Astrology focusing on the sun, moon, and zodiac
7. Astrology without horoscopes
8. Invented by demons
9. Ritual use of blood
10. Evolution/Reincarnation
11. Evolution without karma (no de-evolving)
12. Ghosts, demons, nature spirits
13. Homosexual marriage

Post-Flood Babylon also includes
14. Twelve creator zodiacal gods
15. Many lesser gods/spirits
16. Astrology, fate, magic, and incantations
17. Many different superstitions
18. Original Egyptian, Persian, Canaanite, and Babylonian magic systems were based on this pre-flood version

Sodom and Gomorrah also includes
19. High places were used that included forests and waterfalls
20. Rituals that included sex, dancing, and percussion instruments like the tambourine for a beat
21. Observed four seasonal holidays

Laban's Teraphim also includes
22. Ancestor worship combined with necromancy
23. Magic and astrology with candle ceremonies

The Conjured Spirits

Canaanite Sorcery and Balaam

Canaan, son of Ham, settled in the land of Canaan, later called Israel. His descendants were called the Canaanites. They also inherited this paganism, but added ancestor worship to it. The founders of each Canaanite tribe became the "Baal" and the "Asherah." Baal means "Lord" in Hebrew and Asherah can be translated "the Princess."

In other countries the founders' names were retained. The Assyrians worshiped their founder as the god, Ashur. The Babylonians worshiped Nimrod's son, Mardon, as the god Marduk.

We will define the Canaanite paganism that is described in the Bible by the definitions given in the Babylonian Talmud (Sanhedrin 65).

Forbidden practices
From Deuteronomy we can create a list of nine separate forms of Paganism. Once we identify these and learn exactly what the practices are, we will be able to see the form they occur in today.

> "There shall not be found among you anyone who makes his son or daughter pass through the fire, or who uses divination, or is an observer of times, or an enchanter, or a sorcerer, or a charmer, or one who has a familiar spirit, or a wizard, or a necromancer." *Deuteronomy 18:10-11 (Hebrew)*

Passing Children through Fire
The Canaanites worshiped a god called Moloch with human sacrifices. Children, (mainly their firstborn sons) were burned alive in their sacrifices to this god. This was their way of creating teraphim. See the chapter on

Babylon and Sodom for a detailed description of teraphim.

> "And they have built the high places of Tophet, which is in the valley of the son of Hinnom, to burn their sons and their daughters in the fire…"
> *Jeremiah 7:31*

> "Tophet is Moloch, an idol which was made of brass. The Canaanites heated him from his lower parts; and his outstretched hands were made hot. They put the child in his hands, and it was burnt alive. When the child vehemently cried out the priests beat a drum, so the father would not hear the voice of his son, and move his heart."
> *Rabbi Rashi's Commentary on Jeremiah 7:31*

Diviner – "Kesem"

"Kesem" is the practice where one gazes at an object until he becomes transfixed by it and forgets the world around him. Once he achieves this great level of concentration, he can predict future events. By this definition, some form of meditation is required to achieve an altered state of consciousness. We will see how Balaam did this, shortly.

Observer of Times – "Me'onen"

"Me'onen" is Chaldean Astrology. In later times it was confused with the cloud reader and those who divine by observing the flights of birds.

Enchanter – "Nachash"

The enchanter sees omens in animals. An enchanter uses something to charm/control animals (serpents and scorpions) to be passive or to attack. Burning incense is one way of charming.
Babylonian Talmud: Sanhedrin 65a

Sorcerer – "Kashaph"

"Sorcerer" is a general term for any occult practice. It may include drug use, meditation, or both, but it always has some method to cause an altered state of consciousness. Compare this to Shamanism. The ancient church fathers used the terms "magician" and "sorcerer" interchangeably.

Charmer – "Cheber"

A charmer is one who makes charms. A charm is a piece of jewelry worn for protection or to cause something to happen, such as attract love or money. A protective charm is called an amulet. Other charms are called talismans.

In Acts 19:19, Paul's new Christian converts in the city of Ephesus burned their magic books. Archeology has unearthed some of these texts. The magic rites of Diana included spells, amulets, and talismans invoking her for aid. This is exactly the same thing found today inside the religions of Hinduism and Wicca.

One with a Familiar Spirit – "Ob"

Ob's conjured up ghosts and spirits and made them materialize and speak. One kind used a skull (teraphim) and the other kind used soothsaying. Some rabbis taught that the Ob would see the spirit but not hear it speaking; the inquirer would hear the voice but not see the spirit, while bystanders would not hear or see anything.
Babylonian Talmud: Sanhedrin 65b

> "that other kind of magic, which is supposed to bring up from Hades the souls now resting there, and to exhibit them to public view"
> *Tertullian Treatise on the Soul 57*

Ancient Paganism

The Ob was the kind of Canaanite Sorcerer used by King Saul to conjure the spirit of the prophet Samuel. This event is recorded in 2 Samuel 28.

> "And the woman said unto him, Behold, thou knowest what Saul hath done, how he hath cut off those that have familiar spirits, and the wizards, out of the land: wherefore then layest thou a snare for my life, to cause me to die? And Saul sware to her by the LORD, saying, As the LORD liveth, there shall no punishment happen to thee for this thing. Then said the woman, Whom shall I bring up unto thee? And he said, Bring me up Samuel. And when the woman saw Samuel, she cried with a loud voice: and the woman spake to Saul, saying, Why hast thou deceived me? for thou art Saul. And the king said unto her, Be not afraid: for what sawest thou? And the woman said unto Saul, I saw gods ascending out of the earth. And he said unto her, What form is he of? And she said, An old man cometh up; and he is covered with a mantle. And Saul perceived that it was Samuel, and he stooped with his face to the ground, and bowed himself. And Samuel said to Saul..." *2 Samuel 28:9-15*

So the Ob created what is commonly called a necronomic pit. By use of a teraphim, (her familiar spirit) she caused spirits to appear. This same practice of casting magic circles on the ground for ritual purposes is still used today by modern witches. See the chapter on Wicca for details.

Wizard – "Yidde'oni"
The Talmud states that the name for a wizard, Yidde'oni, comes from a word loosely translated as an extinct animal. It also states that no one remembers exactly what

kind of animal it was. The name carried over to mean those who used a bone of this extinct animal by placing it in their mouths and through some incantations can have the dead speak through this bone. This has been translated as a ventriloquist or a medium.

It is quite possible that the term in this ancient passage means, instead of "extinct animal," a bone from the deceased. Mediums today often ask for an artifact of the deceased in order to try to make some sort of contact with them.

Necromancer – (also translated Dreamers)

A necromancer is a little different from the wizard. According to this passage in the Talmud, necromancers were said to spend nights in cemeteries in order to invoke the spirits of the dead. They would wear special clothing designed especially for this purpose and burn incense to attract the spirits. Once the ritual was thought to be complete, the necromancer would go to sleep on the grave of the deceased, expecting them to appear in their dreams and answer their questions.

Magician/Soothsayer – "Chartumim"

Magician and Soothsayer are general terms for any of the previous practices. A sorcerer uses more ceremonial magic (calling on spirits for aid), while a magician uses more non-ceremonial magic (relying on the power of the human spirit without asking other spirits for aid.) Biblically, whether the occultist thinks he or she is contacting a spirit or using their own power, it is exactly the same demonic manifestation.

Balaam

Balaam was the only recorded prophet in the Bible who used sorcery. He rebelled against God. In these passages we can see he used divination, which required a trance or altered state of consciousness.

> "Angeas said unto Balaam, Conjure for us, I pray thee, with the witchcraft (sorcery), that we may know who will prevail in this battle to which we are now proceeding. And Balaam ordered that they should bring him wax, and he made thereof the likeness of chariots and horsemen representing the army of Angeas and the army of Egypt, and he put them in the cunningly prepared waters that he had for that purpose, and he took in his hand the boughs of myrtle trees, and he exercised his cunning, and he joined them over the water, and there appeared unto him in the water the resembling images of the hosts of Angeas falling before the resembling images of the Egyptians and the sons of Jacob." *Jasher 61:9-10*

> "Zepho said unto Balaam, Try by divination for us that we may know who will prevail in the battle, we or the Egyptians. And Balaam rose up and tried the art of divination, and he was skillful in the knowledge of it, but he was confused and the work was destroyed in his hand. And he tried it again but it did not succeed, and Balaam despaired of it and left it and did not complete it, for this was from the Lord, in order to cause Zepho and his people to fall into the hand of the children of Israel" *Jasher 64:27-29*

Balaam also interpreted dreams correctly, according to Jasher 70:5.

Balaam was called a magician, sorcerer, artificer, and a user of divination. He was not classified as a necromancer, wizard, or one with a familiar spirit. This shows a clear distinction between the two theories of magic.

The theory holds that there are two kinds of magic: ceremonial magic and non-ceremonial magic. Ceremonial magic would be when you do some ritual to make contact with a spirit and then the spirit is supposed to do something for you. Non-ceremonial magic is defined as a human doing a ritual, not to bring up some spirit, but to use the psychic power of his own human spirit.

Name	Description
Sorcerer, magician	General word for an occult practitioner
Non-Ceremonial Magic	
Diviner	Sees the future through trances
Observer of Times	Astrologer
Enchanter	Charms serpents and animals to do his bidding
Charmer	Makes talismans and amulets
Ceremonial Magic	
Wizard	Spirits speak through a possessed medium
Necromancer	Speaks to the dead in his lucid dreams
One with a familiar spirit	Causes a spirit to materialize in a circle (Some use a Teraphim skull).

Pre-Flood Astrology is centered on observing and calculating times. Based on a predetermined set of rules, one would calculate the next time one would be able to contact a god or goddess and work a magic rite. (For instance, a special spell might only work on Halloween or Yule.) This idea is still seen in the myth that, on Halloween, ghosts and spirits are more likely to come back, and are stronger, and magic rites work better.

> "The Horoscope was invented by the Chaldean astrologers." *Hippolytus Heresies 4.3*

Post-Flood Astrology is centered on man and what will happen to him on a daily basis. Astrology was no longer used for predicting the next time a magic rite would work. When the Chaldeans added the horoscope, it then became man-centered. Hippolytus (*Heresies 4.5*) stated if there were any truth in the idea of the horoscope, it would be based on conception – not birth, therefore it must be false.

The idea of astrology was to find out what could happen to a particular person on a specific day. If Mars or Venus was in the right position based on where they were when that person was born, then their finances or love life might improve if they acted today. Or, perhaps, today may or may not be the best time for that person to start a fight or business.

Astrology is based on gods and goddesses who were just men and women long since dead and buried. Doesn't that mean that modern astrology is a joke? Knowing this instantly frees us from being enslaved to it!

Church Father Tatian said it best,

> "Demons invented the concept of fate with astrology to enslave man into worshiping them."
> *Tatian to the Greeks 9*

The other ancient church fathers described astrology in this way:

"The arts of astrologers, soothsayers, augurs, and magicians were made known by the angels who sinned, and are forbidden by God."
Tertullian Apology 35

"Astrology is idolatry." *Tertullian Idolatry 1.9*

"Christians do not employ incantations or spells to perform miracles." *Origen Against Celsus 1:6*

"Christians don't blame fate or stars for their actions." *Tertullian Apology 1*

"Demons... invented astrology, soothsaying, divination, and those productions which are called oracles, necromancy, and the art of magic."
Lactantius Divine Institutes 2:16

"The Church does not perform anything by means of angelic invocations, incantations, or by any other wicked curious art; but, directing her prayers to the Lord." *Irenaeus Against Heresies 2.32*

"God is not to be sought after by means of letters, syllables, and numbers."
Irenaeus Against Heresies 2.25

Priests of Baal

Elijah confronted the priests of Baal on Mount Carmel. Notice the prophet simply prayed to God and his prayer was answered; while the priests of Baal danced in frenzy and cut themselves. This again shows the pagans trying to get into an altered state of consciousness while the true believer just prays.

Baal and Hindu Ashrams

Priests of Baal danced themselves into a frenzy and cut themselves. This kind of meditative technique is called dynamic meditation. This is the same kind of practice performed in Hindu ashrams. The dynamic meditation in the ashrams involves jumping up and down and whirling around with constant movement. Then, all of a sudden at the sound of a bell, all motion stops. This is supposed to throw the practitioner into an altered state of consciousness.

A Magic Circle from the Jewish Kabala
(No different than Canaanite Sorcery)

Paganism in the Middle Ages

Archeology shows the oldest settlements had religions that included the worship of the sun and moon. Later settlements included the other planets. Adding stars as gods came much later.

Sun worship included fire worship and human sacrifice. The counterpart to this was moon worship. Moon worship included water rites. The moon controlled the rising and lowering of the tides.

Later the worship of mother earth and father sky (air or wind) was added. At this point we have what becomes the worship of the four elements. See church father Hippolytus, in book four, for a detailed description of these.

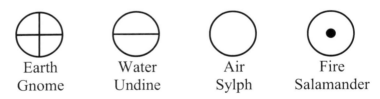

| Earth | Water | Air | Fire |
| Gnome | Undine | Sylph | Salamander |

Pagans started to believe that four types of nature spirits lived in the four elements. Spirits that lived in the earth were referred to as earth spirits or gnomes. Water spirits were called undines. Air spirits were called sylphs and fire spirits were named salamanders.

Ancestor worship added unique gods and goddesses to each religion. Each pagan religion had the worship of the elements as nature spirits. If we trace back the individual names of each spirit from each country, we will find that each one is a kind of "elf" or "fairy."

If we go back another thousand years or so, we will see that elves and fairies were the two different names for the nature spirits.

The following chart shows the names given to the nature spirits in various countries.

Nation	Nature Spirit
Scotland	Brownies, Bogle
England	Fairies, Boggart, Selkie, Shade, Pixies
Norway/Denmark	Dwarf, Elf, Wraith, Hob
China	Hu hsien
Japan	Kappa, Tengu
Laos/Cambodia	Naga
Poland	Domovoi household spirit or teraphim
Germany	Kobolds, Nixie,
Ireland	Leprechaun (Tuatha De Danann), Banshee
Greece/Rome	Dryad, Nymph, Satyr, Kallikantzaros
Scandinavia	Nissen, Tomte, Troll
European Countries	Gnome, Goblin – Bogyman, Hobgoblin, Homunculus, Sprite, Fetch, Pwcca, Pucka, Ogre, Gremlin, Imp

According to some folklore, fairies go all the way back to Tuatha De Danann in Ireland. Geoffrey Keating, in his book entitled *History of Ireland*, states the Formorians were Canaanites who left Canaan because of Noah's curse. They feared that they could not win a war with the sons of Shem so they took to the sea. Formorians were pirates, pillaging the coastal cities. They even observed the pagan festivals back in that time.

It is probable that in Ireland, today's fairies/leprechauns are modern manifestations of the nature spirits from the early Canaanites, which in turn came from the pre-flood pagan religion.

Ancient Paganism

To see just how closely the elves and fairies were connected to the pagan gods, see the chapter on Yule.

Ghosts and Spirits

The ancient church fathers were divided on whether a medium could call up a *real* ghost or if every occurrence was a demon. Turtullian and Philo taught mediums could not call up a real ghost. They believed the creature called up was always a demon imposter.

Justin Martyr, Irenaeus, Origen, and Clement of Alexandria taught there were real ghosts. They taught that most of the time you see or hear a ghost, it would be demonic, but not always. However, all of the ancient church fathers taught you should test the spirits. If they do not confess the true gospel, they are demonic. A Christian can always command a demon imposter to tell the truth and he would have to do so.

> "Moreover, if sorcerers call forth ghosts, and even make what seem the souls of the dead to appear; if they put boys to death, in order to get a response from the oracle; if, with their juggling illusions, they make a pretence of doing various miracles; if they put dreams into people's minds by the power of the angels and demons whose aid they have invited, by whose influence, too, goats and tables (ancient Ouija boards) are made to divine, how much more likely is this power of evil... The wicked spirit, bidden to speak by a follower of Christ, will as readily make the truthful confession that he is a demon." *Tertullian Apology 23*

Paul stated Christians are with the Lord when they die and not roaming the earth.

"Therefore we are always confident, knowing that, whilst we are at home in the body, we are absent from the Lord... We are confident, I say, and willing rather to be absent from the body, and to be present with the Lord." *2 Corinthians 5:6,8*

Jesus told the account of the rich man and Lazarus in Luke 16. In this story the rich man died and instantly opened his eyes in hell. He couldn't get back to earth. After Lazarus died, he was with father Abraham and was unable to return to earth, either.

These verses alone would indicate any "ghost" you come into contact with is, in reality, a demon.

Demons Masquerade as Ghosts

In demonic possession, demons often pretend to be a god or a dead relative. They try to convince others that there is no Hades, no resurrection, and no judgment. We hear the same story among psychics and channelers on television today.

"in cases of exorcism (the evil spirit) affirms himself sometimes to be one of the relatives of the person possessed by him, and sometimes even a god... always making it one of his chief cares to extinguish the very truth which we are proclaiming, that men may not readily believe that all souls remove to Hades, and that they may overthrow faith in the resurrection and the judgment."" *Tertullian Treatise on the Soul 57*

Both the Bible and the ancient church fathers taught us to test the spirits to see if they come from God. Any spirit that tries to convince people that there is no hell, no resurrection, and no judgment is a demon and not a ghost.

The consistent teaching among the church fathers was that at death Christians *immediately* go to be with the Father. Non-Christians go to await the judgment in Hades. The idea of ghosts lingering on earth before going into the "light" was completely unknown to them and is not found anywhere in the Scriptures.

Kabala
In the Middle Ages a book called the Zoar was written by a mystic Jew. This book gave birth to the Kabala. The Kabala is basically Jewish sorcery. The Zoar teaches the doctrine of emanations, also called Lucifer's lie. And it deals heavily with spirits and magic.

Until recently a kabalistic rabbi was considered a heretic. These days, however, the Kabala is considered just another form of Judaism.

Wicca

Halloween

Halloween is the mid-autumn pagan festival. We have seen how the seasonal holy days started with the sons of Noah and spread out to the nations. These festivals became corrupted. Some of the sons of Japheth traveled to France and Germany. See *Ancient Post-Flood History* for detailed analysis showing the migrations of the sons of Noah after the Flood.

The pagan priests in this area of Europe were called Druids. From the religion of the Druids we get the modern practices of Wicca and the celebration of Halloween.

Ancient Halloween

In the chapter on the pagan holy days we learned how the pagan festivals, including Halloween, originated.

Geoffrey Keating wrote in his book, *The History of Ireland* that the early Fomorians were Canaanites who left the land of Canaan because of the curse Noah placed on Canaan. They brought with them the celebration of the eight pagan holy days. The next historical occurrence we see of Halloween is with the inhabitants of Sodom.

"In those days all the people of Sodom and Gomorrah, and of the whole five cities, were exceedingly wicked and sinful against the Lord... And they had in their land a very extensive valley, about half a day's walk, and in it were fountains of water and a great deal of herbage surrounding the water. And all the people of Sodom and Gomorrah went there four times in the year, and with their wives and children and all belonging to them, and they rejoiced with timbrels and dances." *Jasher 18:11-13*

Sodom grew so occultic and immoral that God Himself destroyed that city and the surrounding cities with fire.

"Then the LORD rained upon Sodom and upon Gomorrah brimstone and fire from the LORD out of heaven; And he overthrew those cities, and all the plain, and all the inhabitants of the cities, and that which grew upon the ground."
Genesis 19:24-25

Most Christians are unaware that Halloween is mentioned in the Bible. In Leviticus 23, God ordained a festival, called the Feast of Tabernacles. It was mandatory for representatives of each of the twelve tribes to go up to the Temple in Jerusalem and worship the Lord on this day. The Feast of Tabernacles was observed on the fifteenth day of the seventh month.

After the united kingdom split into Judah and Israel, Jeroboam, the king of the northern kingdom of Israel, did not want his people going to the Temple in the southern kingdom of Judah. Jeroboam said:

"If this people go up to do sacrifice in the house of the LORD at Jerusalem, then shall the heart of this people turn again unto their lord, even unto Rehoboam king of Judah, and they shall kill me, and go again to Rehoboam king of Judah."
1 Kings 12:27

So Jeroboam recreated the calf idols that the Israelites made when they first left Egypt. Jeroboam also recreated the ancient festival of the full moon of the *eighth* month, (or the full moon of October) called Halloween, to be celebrated in Israel in place of the Feast of Tabernacles.

> "Whereupon the king took counsel, and made two calves of gold, and said unto them, It is too much for you to go up to Jerusalem: behold thy gods, O Israel, which brought thee up out of the land of Egypt. And he set the one in Bethel, and the other put he in Dan. And this thing became a sin: for the people went to worship before the one, even unto Dan. And he made an house of high places, and made priests of the lowest of the people, which were not of the sons of Levi. And Jeroboam ordained a feast in the eighth month, on the fifteenth day of the month, like unto the feast that is in Judah, and he offered upon the altar. So did he in Bethel, sacrificing unto the calves that he had made: and he placed in Bethel the priests of the high places which he had made. So he offered upon the altar which he had made in Bethel the *fifteenth day of the eighth month*, even in the month which he had devised of his own heart; and ordained a feast unto the children of Israel: and he offered upon the altar, and burnt incense."
> *1 Kings 12:28-32*

Druids

Most of what we know of Halloween comes from the Druid's religion, sister to witchcraft. In Ireland today it's still known as "oidhch Shamhna" or "Vigil of Samhain." The pagan priesthood of the Druids in Ireland and northwestern Europe believed that Samhain (Sa-ween as it is pronounced), the Lord of the dead (Satan) who controlled the underworld, would gather together all the souls of those who died that year to purge them of their sins. He did this by transmigrating their souls into the bodies of certain animals for a time, a type of Purgatory, before they could go to Druid heaven. He also could be coaxed into giving a lighter sentence by gifts and prayers.

The "harmless" practices observed today in America on Halloween come directly from the ancient practices of the Druids.

BONFIRES: (anciently called Bone Fires) were a form of divination, used to predict what was to come in the following year. A human being or animal was placed in a large wicker basket and burned to death. The pagans believed that the way the victim died and the form of the charred bones, like tea leaf reading, would tell the future for the next twelve months.

BLACK CATS: were supposed to be familiars (spirits who possessed animals and worked with Druids).

JACK-O-LANTERNS: On Halloween night Druids would sacrifice humans to demons to gain more magical power. Jack-o-lanterns were originally made out of turnips, but in America the pumpkin came to be used. These would be used for lanterns. The candle was made partially from the fat of the human victim. Each Jack-o-lantern seen means a loved one had been sacrificially murdered.

TRICK OR TREAT: on Halloween night the people would set food outside to placate the spirits who were always hungry. If you didn't treat them with something they liked, they might be angry and punish (trick) you.

COSTUMES: If you dressed in a costume that represented one of the beings, he might be friendlier and give you more magical power.

Ancient Paganism

Ghosts, goblins, fairies, demons, sprites, and spirits were just some of the beings Druids thought they could contact. Some were supposed to be good, while others were evil. See the chapter on paganism in the Middle Ages for details on various spirits.

Modern History

In the AD 800's, the Pope, in an effort to "Christianize" this pagan holiday, started a mass to be said for all the martyred saints. This was called "All Souls Day" and was held on the first of November. The night before was called All Hallow's Eve. In time the name changed to All Hallow E'en, and finally to Halloween. The pagan practices didn't stop; they simply took on a new form. The bones of the saints were holy, and if you paid great amounts of money, you could touch them and possibly be healed. Then the church started selling other fake relics, and eventually indulgences. If you bought an indulgence, you could go out and sin, because it was paid for in advance. So, if you died, you would still go to heaven. All these things would take place on Halloween. This twisted mixture of Christianity and paganism so outraged one godly man, that he vowed he would change it or die trying. On the Halloween of 1517, Martin Luther nailed 95 theses to the door of the Wittenberg church to protest these and other Roman Catholic dogmas. This marked the date of the beginning of the Protestant Reformation.

Witchcraft is not dead. In England, at the ancient ruins of Stonehenge, Druid priests still perform ancient rites in the same ways their ancestors did. The sacrificing of animals – and, occasionally, – people, is still not uncommon. Even in our time animals are sacrificed on Halloween in Europe and in the Philippines, as well as in the USA.

In the USA, Halloween did not become popular until the mid 1800's when large groups of Irish and Scottish immigrants introduced their specific customs for celebrating Halloween.

In 1965 the satanic bible was first published. Four years later, in 1969, the first church of Satan was formed. With the revival of old Celtic style witchcraft in Missouri and North Carolina, Satanism and witchcraft has been on the rise in the USA.

Witchcraft and sorcery are very real. The number of occult-related murders has been on the increase in this country for more than a generation. One of the most celebrated occult dates is Halloween, and is celebrated in this country on October 31. On college campuses and universities today, Anton LaVey's Satanic bible often out sells the Bible itself!

Paul's Point

Paul warned the Galatian Christians, who were a Celtic people, not to keep their old pagan holidays. Paul seems to wonder if they kept the pagan holidays, Halloween being the chief one, if they were they truly Christian, or did he waste his time preaching to them?

> "However at that time, when you did not know God, you were slaves to those which by nature are no gods. But now that you have come to know God, or rather come to be known by God, how is it that you turn back again to the weak and worthless elemental things, to which you desire to be enslaved all over again? You observe days and months and seasons and years. I fear for you, that perhaps I have labored over you in vain."
> *Galatians 4:8-11 NASB*

Ancient Paganism

If the celebration of Halloween among the Galatian Christians so shocked Paul that he didn't know if they were truly saved, should we be practicing it?

Odin

Yule and Groundhog Day

Yule is the pagan celebration of the winter solstice observed on December 23-25. The ancient Romans practiced Yuletide under the name of Saturnalia. The peoples of Scandinavia began to worship one of their ancestors named Odin as their chief god during Yule. Animals such as dogs, horses, and chickens were sacrificed to the gods and elves; but the worship of Odin required human sacrifice. Lesser items like butter or bread were set out as sacrifices to the elves.

Odin

The most ancient legends describe Odin as a sorcerer who lost one eye while performing a ritual. He became able to see though the eyes of his raven spirit guides. Later, Odin was worshiped as the supreme god.

It should have been obvious if he was a sorcerer and had to do a ritual to obtain this power, that he must not ever have been the original creator god!

In Norse mythology, gods like Odin and the nature spirits (called elves) were worshiped. The gods were no doubt engrafted ancestor worship. Norse mythology divided the universe into nine worlds.

Gods and Elves

The Scandinavians believed the world directly north of the land where humans live is called Álfheimr, meaning land of the elves. Álfheimr is also translated fairyland. This shows a direct connection between elves and fairies. See the chapter on Paganism in the Middle Ages for details on nature spirits. Elves are the nature spirits that supposedly help guide humans to the gods. Directly north of Álfheimr is Asgard, the land of the gods. Asgard was Odin's home and where Valhalla was located.

Ghost Riders

The "Wild Hunt" or "Odin's Hunt" was when the ghost riders would be seen riding though the sky. Gods, elves, and the dead warriors of the past could be seen at Yule. One who sees the sight may be swept along with them to the realm of the dead. Odin would lead the hunt, riding his eight-legged horse named Sleipnir.

The Thin Veil

The Celts consider mid-autumn, or Halloween, to be the time that the veil between worlds is thinnest. It is their New Year's Day. Halloween is the day that the dead may come back to visit, or can be called back by a ritual.

Among the Slavs of Europe the time the veil between worlds is thinnest, their New Years Day, is not mid-autumn, but the winter solstice, or Yule.

The Slavs call it Korochun. It is the time when the black god, Chernobog, and all the evil spirits are at their strongest. A few days later, when the days start getting longer, it is the birth of the new sun, or good god, Koleda.

Yule Conclusion:

It is interesting that from Norse and Slavic paganism we get the elves living in the world right above ours (North Pole) and at Yuletide (Christmas) the veil between the worlds is thinnest so that elves and ghosts may come to visit bringing with them gifts like healing from disease or punishments like death.

The elf spirits were also called Puka. They came to give gifts and healing to those they liked and hurt those they did not like (like putting switches or coal in stockings). The Scandinavians said that when a Puka entered a house, one may hear the greeting of "ho ho ho" from that Puka/elf.

This story, intermingled with the legend of St. Nicholas, a fourth century bishop, formed the legend of Santa Claus. Remember that Santa Claus is supposed to be a "jolly old elf."

It is interesting to see how the Norse god, Odin, changed into Santa. He still comes at Yuletide, or Christmas, but instead of coming on his eight-legged horse, he now rides a sleigh pulled by eight reindeer!

Astaru
In modern times some have tried to bring back the old Norse religion. Today the worship of Odin and Thor is called Astaru.

Groundhog Day
In America, Groundhog Day is celebrated on February 2. The American tradition has it that the groundhog will emerge from its burrow on that day. If it sees its shadow, there will be six more weeks of winter; but if it does not see its shadow, spring will come early.

As we learned in the chapter about the pagan holy days, February 2 is mid-winter and the pagans call this day Imbolc. On Imbolc the Irish Celts celebrated the Feast of Brigid. The goddess Brigid was a diviner and predicted the weather. The Scottish goddess celebrated on this day was called Bride. Both these goddesses were fire goddesses. The animals that were special to these goddesses were the animals that hibernated during the winter. Among the Scotts it was said:

"Early on Bride's morn the serpent shall come from its hole." *Scottish folklore*

In Scotland the serpent foretold when the fire goddess would bring spring. In other countries it was other hibernating animals like the badger, the hedgehog, or the bear.

When German immigrants brought this tradition to America, the groundhog became the choice animal for the herald of spring.

Later the medieval Christian church created Saint Brigid and combined much of the trappings of the goddess Brigid with these celebrations. February 2, for example, was kept as her day but the name was changed to Candlemas. The medieval church saying goes:

"If Candlemas be fair and bright, winter has another flight. If Candlemas brings clouds and rain, winter will not come again."
Medieval Christian tradition

Saint Brigid's Cross is still a powerful symbol among Wiccans today. See the chapter on Wicca for details.

One Celtic custom was to leave a white cloth hanging on the front door on the evening of February 1. The next morning if the cloth was marked, then Brigid passed by that night and blessed the house.

Wicca and Hinduism

Wicca, also called Witchcraft, is a pagan religion from medieval Europe, thought to have come through the Celtic tribes migrating into Europe from the Middle East around 700 BC.

Most religions are based on a specific writing or holy book, which tells followers how to practice their religion. Christianity – the Bible; Islam – The Koran; Buddhism – the Pali texts; etc. Unlike these, Wicca has no written guide or holy book. Each group of Wiccans, usually called a coven, writes its own code in what is called a book of shadows. This means many who call themselves witches actually teach conflicting views.

A large number of Wiccans teach their religion is nearly identical with that of Druidism, which did not leave any written records, either. The basic teachings of Wicca are just like those of pre-flood paganism.

Sabbats and Esbats
The eight pagan holy days are celebrated by Wiccans, Druids, and other pagans alike. The four mid-seasonal days are referred to as Sabbats. The four lesser days, the solstices and equinoxes, are called Esbats. See the chapter on the Pagan Holy Days for details on how these got started and were adapted by pagans.

God
There was a god or power that anciently created everything. Since it did this by putting itself into creation, it no longer exists and, of course, no one remembers what it was. We (and all life) are from it and therefore are evolving into gods.

Evolution and Reincarnation

Wiccans teach we are continuing to evolve into gods through a process of evolution and reincarnation. The Hindus believe in karma, which means if a man lives an evil life he will downgrade in his next reincarnation. He may come back as an animal. In Wicca there is no concept of karma. You will either learn your lesson and advance or will come back and do this life over again until you get it right. We will see this Wiccan concept was taught among the first century Gnostics in a later chapter.

Magic Powers

Since we are evolving to what the creator once was, some of us who are more advanced than others will display godlike powers. These are referred to as psychic powers.

Spirits

The real spirits out there are nature spirits, usually called elementals by Wiccans, and are our ancestors evolving into more powerful gods. We have learned about the concept of nature spirits or elementals and the worship of ancestors/teraphim.

Thoughtforms

Since we are the highest form of god, if a large group of people worship a particular god, over time the energy expended from their worship actually creates a living entity. This is called a thoughtform. We create the gods we worship. This same concept of thoughtforms is taught in Tibetan Buddhism.

Since most Wiccans do not believe in a literal devil or demons, their explanation for when new practitioners see demons or get possessed, is that they have crossed over from reality and entered the world of thoughtforms unknowingly. This is a brilliant tactic of Lucifer. Even though Wiccans see demons, they don't believe in them!

Rituals, Spells and Circles
A Wiccan ritual consists of drawing a magic circle on the ground and then in ritual form gathering power from the people. If enough people are present or gathering power from a god or goddess thoughtform, the spell taps into the energy that all the flowers of the god or goddess had put into it over the centuries. It has been explained as a kind of giant cosmic battery. In Wicca this process is called "drawing down the moon."

We have learned from the chapter on Canaanite sorcery the ancient Canaanite sorcerers cast circles on the ground in order to bring up spirits. This is the very same practice.

Wiccan Tools
Creating charms is also part of the craft. A protective charm is called an amulet. A charm to cause you to receive something good is called a talisman. Pagans make use of charms, candles, incense, color and sex magic and other occultic devices. The ceremonial knife used in rituals is called an athame. The handle of the knife is either black (for black magic) or white (for white magic).

Degrees in the Craft
As you learn the concepts and learn to practice the craft you go up in degrees. In the USA there are three degrees. Once you achieve the third degree in American witchcraft, you have become adept at casting circles and practicing magic and have chosen a new name for yourself. After you have been initiated into the craft by taking an oath that you will hold the craft superior to all other religions, you are told to go meditate and find your spirit guide.

Ancient Paganism

 These first three degrees in the American tradition equal the first degree of the Celtic style of witchcraft. All that they will tell you at this point is that when you are deemed ready by your spirit guide you will receive a new magic name only for you and your spirit guide to know. From that point on they do not talk about the second or third Celtic degrees.

The following is a chart that compares ancient Celtic witchcraft with Christianity.

Witchcraft	Christianity
Jesus is just a thought form	Jesus is God in human form
Satan is just a bad thought form	Satan is a real, living fallen angel
Reincarnation	Resurrection
Evolution	Special Creation
There are many gods (thought forms)	There is only one God
We make gods	The one true God made us
We are becoming gods. The spark of the original god is in each one of us	God is distinct from creation. We will never be God
ESP, psychic powers	Prayer
Spiritism	Demonology
We heal ourselves by visualizing	God heals us if He wills, by prayer

Notice how Wiccan thought has crept into the church in some denominations. Some say Jesus is not God, or Satan is not real. Some denominations do not believe in the physical resurrection and even some Christian cults teach reincarnation. Some churches have accepted evolution, our magic power of confession, even to the extent that we are little gods. Some have begun to replace prayer with meditation. See the Word Faith and Emergent section for details.

Legends

There are legends of an ancient practice among the Wiccans about a god/man/king whose ritual death brought life to the crops. If Wicca is simply an offshoot of Druidism and Druidism an offshoot from the religion of the Jewish patriarchs mixed with the paganism of Baal, we can see why the further back we go, the more similar it is to ancient history.

Hinduism and Buddhism

Hinduism's fundamental principles are the same as that of Wicca. Notable differences are:

Some of the original creator god/force still exists. But Hinduism agrees with Wicca in that it is an impersonal force. Hinduism even gives a name to the idea that the human spirit is a divine emanation. They call it the "Atman." Wicca teaches this concept but does not have a name for it.

Buddhism goes a step farther in saying that consciousness is an illusion. Buddhists seek to lose this illusion and to go back to being a part of this creator force. In other words, they seek to go back to the "nothingness" from which they came.

Tibetan Buddhism is headed by the Dali Lama. This form of Buddhism combines the general Buddhist teachings with shamanism and other occultic teachings like Tantra and the creation of thoughtforms.

Satanism

True Satanism has always believed the lie and followed Lucifer into godhood. Historically this has been the case with Aleister Crowley and his organization the OTO, and with MacGregor Mathers and his organization the Golden Dawn, and with many others.

Today we have groups such as Anton LaVey and his Church of Satan which describe themselves as religious Satanists. This basically means that modern psychology has influenced this group. Instead of believing in *real* spirits, they think the spirits are just part of their own subconscious mind. Crazy isn't it? Mixing psychology with occultism makes them atheistic magicians!

All these occult groups have some form of meditation and belief in becoming gods. Hindus call mediation Yoga Sutra, but Buddhism refers to it at Prana. Shamans and Native Americans use the term Vision Quests when talking about their meditative practices.

Pagan Religions Compared
The following chart compares present day world religions and the teachings from the great apostasy.

The first column is the name of the religion. If the second column is checked, it means that religion practices magic. Notice Christianity, Judaism, and Islam are the only religions that forbid the practice of magic. There are, however, cults inside of each of these three religions that practice some forms of paganism. These are the Islamic dervishes, the Jewish kabala, and the Christian mystics.

The next three columns indicate if the religion believes the creator still exists but is impersonal, the creator no longer exists, or the creator exists and is a personal intelligent being. Notice again only Christianity, Judaism, and Islam believe in a personal God.

If the fifth column is checked, the religion believes in multiple gods. If the sixth column is checked, the religion specifically teaches the doctrine of emanations, that we call Lucifer's lie. If the last column is checked, the religion believes in reincarnation.

	Mag	CEF	CNF	CEP	MG	Em	Re
Buddhism	✓		✓				✓
Confucianism	✓	✓					✓
Druidism	✓				✓		✓
Hinduism	✓	✓			✓	✓	✓
Jainism	✓			✓		✓	✓
Kabala	✓	✓			✓	✓	
Shamanism	✓				✓		✓
Shinto	✓	✓			✓		✓
Sikh	✓					✓	
Sufi	✓					✓	✓
Tao	✓	✓					✓
Voodoo	✓			✓	✓		
Wicca	✓		✓		✓	✓	✓
Zoroastrianism	✓			✓	✓		
Christianity				✓			
Islam				✓			
Judaism				✓			

Mag = Belief in Magic,
CEF = The Creator exists but is an impersonal force
CNF = The Creator does not exist, but was an impersonal force
CEP = The Creator exists and is a person
MG = Multiple gods/creators
Em = There is an Emanation of the original Creator God in each of us
Re = Reincarnation

Now let's take a look at the tools used today by modern occultists.

Doorways to the Demonic World

Occultic Tools

The following modern-day occult practices can be identified by ancient sources.

Divination
Divination is defined as a practice of trying to tell the future. It differs from prophecy in that a prophecy is given when God directly reveals coming events to a prophet. No divination or meditation is involved.

As explained in earlier chapters, there is ceremonial magic and non-ceremonial magic. The same applies to the practice of divination. Ceremonial divination tools are used to allow a practitioner to communicate with spirits. Hopefully, the spirit can tell them about the future. Non-ceremonial divination is used when practitioners supposedly learn to use their own power to see the future.

Ceremonial Divination Tools:
Ceremonial tools include Ouija boards, channeling, séances, and automatic writing. These are the tools everyone agrees that they need help from the spirits with.

Non-Ceremonial Divination Tools:
Non-ceremonial tools include Tarot cards, tea leaf reading, runes, astrology, I Chang, palmistry, divining rods (water witching), crystal balls, pendulum scrying, and the black mirror. These are tools that some think work by the power of the human spirit. Contact with spirits is not necessary.

Meditation
None of these tools work without some form of meditation. Varying forms of mediation include:

trances, yoga, transcendental meditation, TM sidhi, Reiki, astral projection, Zen, hypnosis, and pyramid power.

Meditative Effects

Being in a meditative state can supposedly give the ability to use psychic healing and develop psychic powers like clairvoyance (the ability to see visions), clairsentience (the ability to obtain knowledge by touching an object), clairaudience (the ability to hear voices of spirits), telepathy (the ability to read people's thoughts), and psychokenesis (the ability to move physical objects with your mind).

Automatic Writing

Automatic writing is defined as when a spirit takes control of a person's hand and causes them to write down on paper what that spirit wants to communicate. An offshoot of this is graphology, commonly known as handwriting analysis.

Black Mirror

The Black Mirror is actually water scrying. It is done by filling a bowl with water and putting a few drops of black ink into the water to make the water completely dark. Then, after some incantations, a person stares into the blackness until they see a vision. This is a favorite form of divination among many Wiccans today.

Other Magic Practices

Other practices include the invocation of angels and demons, casting circles, magic rituals, color magic, and casting spells. Some objects used in these practices are prayer beads, candles, stones and crystals, and jewelry in the form of amulets and talismans.

Astral Projection

Astral Projection is the idea that people are simply spirits inside the human body. Therefore a person can, through a type of meditation, learn to disconnect their spirit from their body and roam around on earth and in other dimensions, talk to spirit beings, and then return safely to their body.

When I was still in high school and a very young Christian, I went to a roller skating party with my friend, Mike. While we were there I met a man who claimed he could astral project. I scoffed at first until I saw him do something to another kid, kind of like he was hypnotizing him or something. I talked to the occultist for a while about the process of astral projection. I asked him to prove it was real to me. He told me to give him about 45 minutes to go home and get into a meditative sleep and he would come and materialize to my friend and me. We waited about an hour but nothing happened.

The party was over so we decided to go home. We drove though a fog on the way back to Mike's house. It made us both a little nervous. So we pulled over and I asked Mike to agree with me in prayer. He agreed and I prayed something like this:

> "Father, we ask your protection for us tonight. You know what has happened and about the man we met tonight. We pray that if he is of You and does these things though Your power, or if he simply has this power in himself, we ask that you let us know for sure. If this power is a good thing we would like to learn how to use it, too. But, if this is a trick of Satan we ask you to bind Satan and let us know that for sure, too. We love you Father, and pray in Jesus name. Amen."

Ancient Paganism

We waited a few minutes and the fog went away, so I drove back to his house, dropped him off, and went home and got some sleep. About two weeks later I saw that occultist again. I asked him if he tried to find us and materialize to us or if he had forgotten, because we never saw anything.

He told me he went home, meditated and left his body. He said he had some trouble finding us, but then he saw us in my father's yellow truck, pulled off to the side of the road. He approached the truck and all of a sudden everything went black for him. He couldn't find his way anywhere, so he finally gave up and went back. I asked him if that had ever happened to him before. He said it had never happened before and he had no idea what exactly did take place.

That experience taught me two things that night. One, astral projection was not real. It is a Satanic counterfeit. Second, it taught me my Lord loves me so much that He protected me and answered my prayer in less than five minutes!

Years later I discovered the ancient church fathers believed the same thing. Origen, in his work *Against Celsus 3:31* said he believed astral projection is not possible, but simply a trick of demons.

Suzy's Tarot Cards and Astrology Program
I had a friend who got heavily involved with reading Tarot cards. She read everything she could on the subject and practiced readings all the time. She became a little depressed because she was never very accurate in her readings. She began to research it more deeply and found a man who lived in Kansas City who was supposed to be one of the world's leading authorities on Tarot cards.

Suzy went to see him and explained her problem to him. She said she followed the ritual, had all the words memorized, and did everything *exactly* like the books said she should, but to no avail.

He explained that you can't just say a few words, invoke a spirit, wave your hands and say abracadabra, and expect it to work. He explained the Tarot deck was just a tool to use to get information. The *real* power behind the cards comes from the spirits. To be effective she needed to learn to meditate and tap into these forces.

Suzy did not like that answer. She gave up on Tarot cards and decided to get into astrology. She figured that if she had a computer plot all the positions of the stars and planets, the computer would be so accurate she couldn't fail. When she discovered she had the same problem, she found another "expert" and went to see that lady.

Suzy told her about her Tarot cards experience and the computer astrology program. She asked if there was a better computer program, one that was more accurate. She was very surprised to hear the astrological expert say that the problem was not the computer program. She was sure the computer program was accurate enough. This lady used a very similar program for her charts.

She said Suzy's problem was that she did not realize that astrology was just a tool to read people. To be accurate with it, she must learn to meditate and tap into the spiritual energies around her.

Suzy sat there for a moment. Then she told the lady that explanation didn't make sense to her. If she used a Ouija board, of course it wouldn't work unless a spirit was there to move the pointer. But if astrology worked – if events were pre-ordained, then a computer program should be nearly 100% accurate with or without any spirits or meditation involved! The lady simply responded "that's just not how it works."

I do not know where Suzy is today, but I pray for her salvation.

Suzy's experiences taught me a very valuable lesson. All these occult paraphernalia are just tools. None of them really work by themselves. But all these tools require practitioners to get in touch with demonic spirits though meditation. One tool is just as good as the other. In other words, none of them really work!

Paganism's Influence
on the Church

Biblical Practices

By now some questions should come to mind: aren't some of the practices in the Bible meditative or occultic? Aren't there some objects that have occult power? If not, what's the difference?

We will look at these individually and see what the Bible really says about them.

We will examine the Magi's visit to Jesus, the Urim and Thummim, Paul's being caught up (or astral projecting), Saul using a medium to contact a ghost, speaking in tongues, worship in the church today, healing by the laying on of hands, Elijah's bones, the brazen serpent, the ark of the covenant, Paul's handkerchiefs, communion and transubstantiation, prophetic dreams and visions, and the spiritual gift of discernment.

Didn't the Magi use astrology to find Jesus?
No. The word Magi originally meant astrologer, but in Persia came to mean wise man or ruler. The Magi who visited Jesus were Persians who had copies of the prophecies of Balaam.

> "The Magi that visited Jesus were Persians not Chaldeans." *Origin Against Celsus 1.58*

> "The Magi had a copy of the prophecies of Balaam." *Origin Against Celsus 1.60*

Julius Africanus wrote in his work, *The Narrative of the Events Happening in Persia During the Birth of Christ*, that the king of Persia had a dream that the statues of the Persian gods fell down in their temple. A voice told him they were deceivers and the true God had been born in

Judea. He awoke and conferred with Magi, who confirmed that a star appeared as prophesied by Balaam. He then dispatched the Magi. When they came to Jerusalem they had to ask where the new king was to be born because they did not have a copy of Micah's prophesies. They found baby Jesus based on the Scriptures, not astrology.

When they returned, they told about the Christ child and brought a picture that one of their artists had painted of Jesus sitting on Mary's knee.

Wasn't the Urim & Thummim a form of divination?

No. Both Josephus and the Talmud (Yoma 73:71) give a detailed description on how the Urim and Thummim worked. If God wanted to communicate with the priest, the Urim would glow. Only then could he ask a "yes" or "no" question. If the answer was "yes" the Thummim would glow. The Talmud states in *Sotah 48* that following the destruction of the First Temple, the Urim and Thummim ceased to be used, and could not be used again until 'the dead are raised and the Messiah ben David will come.' The Talmud also records that the Urim and Thummim, the ark of the covenant, eternal fire, and the holy oil for anointing the priests were not in the Second Temple. (Horayot 3, Sheet 47). Rabbi Maimonides stated this happened because the high priests no longer possessed the Holy Spirit.

Didn't the apostle Paul use astral projection?

No. As recorded in 2 Corinthians 12, Paul either saw a vision or died for a short time after he was stoned and left for dead. God started the process. There was not any meditation on Paul's part. Origen, in his work *Against Celsus 3:31*, said he believes astral projection is not possible, but simply a trick of demons.

If Saul used a medium to contact Samuel, can't I use one to contact a saint?

No. Saul was put to death by the Lord for doing this.

> "So Saul died for his transgression which he committed against the LORD, even against the word of the LORD, which he kept not, and also for asking counsel of one that had a familiar spirit, to enquire of it" *1 Chronicles 10:13*

> "Those who make prayers to the dead will suffer for their impiety and rebellion against God since this is an unforgivable rite and a violation of sacred law." *Lactantius 7.67*

Doesn't speaking in tongues and worshiping God require you to be in an altered state of consciousness?

No, look at Acts 2. The apostles were praying and the Holy Spirit came upon them. The Holy Spirit came in His own way and in His own time. The Apostles began to praise God and preach the gospel. This time it just happened to be in other languages as the Spirit directed.

Doesn't healing require special holy oil and the laying on of hands to transfer healing energies to someone?

The oil is not special. It's just regular oil, and even though elders lay their hands on the person prayed for, there is no meditation involved. Even the Wiccans will tell you prayer is totally different from meditation and casting spells with incantations. See the chapter on Wicca for full details.

Didn't Elisha's bones contain a residual power that resurrected a dead man?

No. The prophet Elisha requested a double portion of the spirit of Elijah. The Holy Spirit performed eight miracles through Elijah before his rapture. The Holy Spirit had preformed only 15 miracles though Elisha before his death; Elisha was one miracle short. So, to fulfill the prophecy, the Holy Spirit performed one more miracle though Elisha's body after his death.

Didn't the Israelites think there was power in the brazen serpent and use it in a ritual?

Yes, some did. When godly king Hezekiah heard this was going on, he had the brazen serpent destroyed. The idea that relics contain power to heal amounts to idolatry; and the practice of idolatry is a sin before God. See 2 Kings 18 for details.

Didn't the ark of the covenant contain power to perform miracles and kill those who touched it?

Not exactly. The miracles happened when the presence of God was in and around the ark. It was the power of God that performed the miracles, not the power of the ark. It never killed the godly that were supposed to touch it, just those that were forbidden to go near it. Again it was the power of God's presence, not an occult power in the ark itself.

Didn't Paul put some kind of occult power into handkerchiefs to heal people who touched them?

The Bible *does* say that Paul healed in an unusual way by giving out handkerchiefs. But it does not say he used the occult, meditated, nor did any kind of ritual over them to achieve this effect. The ancient church was very clear on this point.

"The Church does not perform anything by means of angelic invocations, or incantations, or by any other wicked curious art; but, directing her prayers to the Lord." *Irenaeus Against Heresies 2.32*

Doesn't the communion bread and wine turn into the body and blood of Christ when blessed by the priest?

No. Communion is a memorial of what the Lord Jesus Christ has done for us, not a magical transformation. If this were true, the priest would be guilty of murdering our God. Ancient church father Irenaeus said the church never taught what is now called the doctrine of Transubstantiation and that it is a demonic doctrine taught by Gnostics.

> "Pretending to consecrate cups mixed with wine, he [The Gnostic Marcus] contrives to give them a purple and reddish color, so that Charis [the Holy Spirit], should be thought to drop her own blood into that cup through means of his invocation... the church has never taught such a thing... all who follow such a demonic teaching are crack-brained." *Irenaeus Against Heresies 1.13*

What about prophetic dreams and visions? Isn't sleep a kind of altered state of consciousness?

No, the prophet Daniel, for example, prayed and asked God to reveal a prophecy to him in a dream. Then, he went into a natural sleep and God performed this miracle. He did not do a ritual and meditate into an altered state of consciousness.

Didn't some of the prophets go into trance to be able to prophesy?

No, the Word of the Lord came to them and spoke with them while they were in their right mind. Only Balaam used what we would call a trance to prophecy; and when he prophesied this way, the process was called sorcery.

Didn't the apostle Peter use meditative trances?
Some English translations do use the word trance in Acts
10:11 and 11:5. In context it is clear that Peter was
praying in the Christian way and God showed him a
vision. He did not do any kind of meditation or use drugs
to hear from God.

**If drug use is sorcery, doesn't that mean doctors and
medicine are sorcery and therefore forbidden?**
No. In reaction to the Gnostic sorcery and magic potions,
the heretic Tatian started teaching that it was a sin to take
any drug for any reason. He taught even taking medicine
is evil and shows you do not have faith in God. We see
these false teachings today in many cults like Christian
Science, Mind Science, and others.

The ancient church fathers taught the opposite. They said
medicine is not demonic and herbs were created by God
for the use of men. This following quote is from the Old
Testament Apocrypha but was often quoted among the
ancient church fathers for its wisdom.

"Honor the physician with the honor due him,
according to your need of him, for the Lord
created him; for healing comes from the Most
High, and he will receive a gift from the king...
The Lord created medicines from the earth, and a
sensible man will not despise them. Was not water
made sweet with a tree in order that his power
might be known? And he gave skill to men that he
might be glorified in his marvelous works. By
them he heals and takes away pain; the pharmacist
makes of them a compound. His works will never
be finished; and from him health is upon the face
of the earth... And give the physician his place,
for the Lord created him; let him not leave you,

> for there is need of him. There is a time when success lies in the hands of physicians, for they too will pray to the Lord that he should grant them success in diagnosis and in healing, for the sake of preserving life. He who sins before his Maker, may he fall into the care of a physician."
> *Sirach 38:1-2,4-8, 12-15*

So, although using meditation and drugs to alter you state of mind is sorcery and a sin before God, using medicine is not sorcery.

Isn't the gift of discernment the same thing as developing psychic powers to be spiritually sensitive?
No. The Holy Spirit gives this gift to enable a believer to discern between the truth of God and a satanic lie. Since the Holy Spirit is both the author of the Bible and the giver of the "gift of discernment," this gift should be telling the believer the same truths taught in Scripture. Since the Bible refers to psychic powers and mediation as sorcery, which is simply a satanic counterfeit, then the gift of discernment should be showing you the same truths.

How do we know the biblical way of prophesying is any better than the pagan way?
The pagan way is called sorcery and is forbidden by God. Notice that there has never been a pagan prophecy book written that contains a series of prophecies that came to pass exactly as prophesied with 100% accuracy. None of the false religions have a series of prophetic visions that came to pass. Only the Bible contains such a list.

The Bible records a continual stream of prophecy starting with the pre-flood world and continuing through our time. The rebirth of the nation of Israel was the starting point for a whole series of newly fulfilled prophecies. Even the exact time, place, and circumstances for her rebirth were prophesied in great detail. Since 1948 AD, there have been over 53 prophecies fulfilled. The Bible lists another fifteen to come in the very near future. With a record like that, the answer should be obvious. See the book *Ancient Prophecies Revealed* for details.

Conclusion

It is a trick of Satan to say occult sensitivity is the same thing as the biblical gift of discerning of spirits. All the gifts of the Spirit are achieved by God working though you, not your starting a process though meditation. The Bible describes meditative practices as sorcery and these activities are forbidden. None of the prophets used mediation, except for the pseudo-prophet and sorcerer, Balaam, and none of the relics mentioned in the Bible had any kind of power in and of themselves.

Serpent Meditation

Prayer vs Meditation

The first century Gnostics combined meditation with prayer. The ancient church fathers condemned this practice but later the Desert Fathers re-embraced this form of Gnosticism.

Jesus said not to pray like the hypocrites do, so that men will respect them, nor like the Gentiles do, with meaningless repetitions (or mantras) to be respected by the spirits. He said to pray intelligently, to be respected by God. He then gave the Lord's Prayer as a model.

> "When you pray, you are not to be like the hypocrites; for they love to stand and pray in the synagogues and on the street corners so that they may be seen by men. Truly I say to you, they have their reward in full... And when you are praying, do not use meaningless repetition as the Gentiles do, for they suppose that they will be heard for their many words." *Matthew 6:5,7*

Paul said prayer is making your requests known to God, not emptying your mind. The ancient church fathers said the same:

> "The Church does not perform anything by means of angelic invocations, or incantations, or by any other wicked curious art; but, directing her prayers to the Lord." *Irenaeus Against Heresies 2.32*

> "Mature Christians pray only to God, without thought for bodily position or set time and their prayers are not selfish."
> *Clement of Alexandria, Stromata book 7.7*

Ancient Paganism

The ancient church fathers taught that when the Holy Spirit comes upon a Christian and the gifts of the Spirit are manifested, it is done with clarity of mind. In contrast, a person praying a satanic counterfeit prayer goes into an altered sate of consciousness, called an "ecstasy," where they are not in control of themselves.

> "A true prophet under the control of the Holy Spirit does not fall into ecstasy or madness like the pagans do." *Origen Against Celsus 7:3*

Therapeute
The Therapeute were the first Christian monastic sect in Alexandria, Egypt, which formed shortly after Mark's arrival there. They mixed Christian prayer with a corrupt form of Essene meditation/prayer. See *Eusebieus 2.17* and *Josephus Antiques 15.10.5 & 17.13.3; War 2.8.2,3,6* for details.

Eastern meditation is the "meaningless repetition" that Jesus said the Gentiles did. A perfect example of this is transcendental meditation. The idea is not a *conscious* asking of a request and thanking God for His blessings, but emptying of the mind, in order to be put it into an altered state of consciousness.

The ancient church fathers call this altered state of consciousness "ecstasy." Instead of relying on the Holy Spirit to speak, the error was that they created a state of ecstasy to commune with a spirit that they *thought* was God. Let's look at how the great heretic Montanus did this.

Montanus
According to the testimony of the early church fathers Irenaeus, Tertullian, Hippolytus, and Eusebius, Montanus

wrote the book "The New Prophecy" in which he taught the following:

Montanus himself was the "other" comforter that Jesus said would come. He brought with him a new form of prophecy. In this new kind of prophecy, a "vain babbling" was used to alter a person's consciousness so that he could channel the "Holy Spirit." We see here again the use of meaningless words, or mantras, to get into this state of consciousness.

The ancient church fathers said this new form of prophecy only brought false prophecies. They also said that "vain babbling" was never practiced by any Old Testament or New Testament prophet or teacher.

Eusebius describes the "ecstasy" as a false system that does away with the *real* spiritual gifts since it circumvents the Holy Spirit to reach another spirit.

"Montanists set at nought the gift of the Spirit, which in the latter times has been, by the good pleasure of the Father, poured out upon the human race, do not admit that aspect of the evangelical dispensation presented by John's Gospel, in which the Lord promised that He would send the Paraclete (John 16); but set aside at once both the Gospel and the prophetic Spirit. Wretched men indeed! who wish to be pseudo-prophets, forsooth, but who set aside the gift of prophecy from the Church. We must conclude, moreover, that the Montanists can't admit the Apostle Paul either. For, in his Epistle to the Corinthians, he speaks expressly of prophetical gifts, and recognizes men and women prophesying in the Church. Sinning, therefore, in all these particulars, against the Spirit of God." *Irenaeus Against Heresies 3.11 – AD 178*

Here Tertullian is quoted as saying the "ecstasy" is not being in your right mind and sometimes being completely unconscious.

"The Montanist book, 'The New Prophecy' teaches when God speaks through man a 'grace ecstasy or rapture' is imparted whereby he necessarily loses his sensation because he is overshadowed with the power of God." *Tertullian Marcion 4.22*

"Thus in the very beginning sleep was inaugurated by ecstasy: 'And God sent an ecstasy upon Adam, and he slept.'" *Tertullian Treatise of the Soul 1.45*

"Montanus became beside himself, and being suddenly in a sort of frenzy and ecstasy, he raved, and began to babble and utter strange things, prophesying in a manner contrary to the constant custom of the Church handed down by tradition from the beginning. Some of those who heard his spurious utterances at that time were indignant, and they rebuked him as one that was possessed, and that was under the control of a demon, and was led by a deceitful spirit, and was distracting the multitude; and they forbade him to talk, remembering the distinction drawn by the Lord and his warning to guard watchfully against the coming of false prophets. But others imagining themselves possessed of the Holy Spirit and of a prophetic gift, were elated and not a little puffed up; and forgetting the distinction of the Lord, they challenged the mad and insidious and seducing

spirit, and were cheated and deceived by him. In consequence of this, he could no longer be held in check, so as to keep silence. Thus by artifice, or rather by such a system of wicked craft, the devil, devising destruction for the disobedient, and being unworthily honored by them, secretly excited and inflamed their understandings which had already become estranged from the true faith."
Eusebius Ecclesiastical History 5.16-17

Ancient church father Eusebius went on to report that the leaders of the church after studying the "babbling spirit" and the prophecies that did not come to pass, judged it to be the work of a "false and seducing spirit" and they separated themselves from the heretics and withheld communion from them. To prove that a true prophet does not "speak in ecstasy" Eusebius says, in chapter 17:

"The false prophet falls into an ecstasy which is 'purposed ignorance' or 'involuntary madness of soul' But they cannot show that one of the old or one of the new prophets was thus carried away in spirit. Not Agabus, or Judas, or Silas, or the daughters of Philip, or Ammia in Philadelphia, or Quadratus, or any others."
Eusebius Ecclesiastical History 5.17

Eusebius also stated if they were real prophets, their predictions would always be 100% accurate, because "the apostle thought it necessary that the prophetic gift should continue in all the Church until the final coming. But they (Monanists) cannot show it."

So the real gifts of the Spirit (prophecy, healing, miracles, etc.) will continue until the Second Coming of our Lord Jesus; but those who try to force these experiences end up touching the demonic. One ancient church father reported that's how Montanus and Maximilla died, at the hands of a demon.

> "The 'maddening spirit' caused Montanus to hang himself. A few years later it caused Maximillia to commit suicide in the same way."
> *Asterius Urbanus 3.2*

Even though this practice was condemned by the ancient church fathers, it was adopted a few hundred years later by what are called the Desert Fathers. These were some of the first monks. We get things like the Gregorian chants and Ignatius de Loyola's "spiritual exercises" from their form of Christian mysticism.

Other things that help create an "ecstasy" or "center your mind" are breath prayers, borrowed from the Buddhists, and labyrinth walks. Anything that is repetitive enough can cause an "ecstasy." When Elijah confronted the priests of Baal, they were dancing in a frenzy and cutting themselves. This was their way of causing an ecstasy.

In Ezekiel 8, Ezekiel wrote that the Temple priests created stations in the Temple with icons of creeping things and other symbols, and had sunrise services. This can be seen in churches today as prayer stations, many having icons of saints and Mary. In each station the object, or idol, is stared at long enough to create an ecstasy. In Ezekiel 13-15 we see this practice led to false prophecies or "lying divinations." God said anyone who went to the idolatrous priest for council would suffer the same fate as those priests. This is a very real warning for us today, to stay away from churches that practice contemplative prayer, or have stations with images or idols in their churches. If you do not stay far away, you *will* suffer for it in the future!

The ancient church fathers warned against the Carpocratian Gnostics, who had idols of Jesus, various saints, angels, Aristotle, Pythagoras, and others, which they would adorn with wreaths and garlands. They were the first to venerate icons, and were sternly rebuked for this practice.

In the mid twentieth century we saw a formula for creating an ecstasy from the Latter Rain Movement. At the beginning of the twenty-first century we saw another formula for creating an ecstasy from the Contemplative Prayer Movement. In many cases meditation causes one to form the opinion that he or she is divine. We will see the ultimate form of this in the Antichrist's religion when he declares that he really *is* God.

Kundalini Meditation, also called Serpent Meditation, eventually brings "enlightenment," where you realize you are god. Apparently other kinds of meditation cause the practitioners to come to the same conclusion. They may say we are not god; but god is *in* everything. This is just another way of saying the exact same thing. It is still Lucifer's lie, the Kabalistic Emanation Doctrine.

Jesus said in the end times many would come and say they had, what we would call, the Christ consciousness.

> "For many shall come in my name, saying, I am Christ; and shall deceive many." *Mark 13:6*

Even though they may do miracles in Jesus' name, they are not His.

Ancient Paganism

> "Many will say to me in that day, Lord, Lord, have we not prophesied in thy name? and in thy name have cast out devils? and in thy name done many wonderful works? And then will I profess unto them, I never knew you: depart from me, ye that work iniquity." *Matthew 7:22-23*

These people are deceived by seducing spirits. To be seduced means you have been manipulated into doing something you think is right; but the outcome benefits the seducer and harms the one seduced.

Jesus said not to look for Him in the inner rooms or the desert places (Matthew 24:23-26). The "inner rooms" could refer to looking inward in meditation for a Christ consciousness. The term "mantra" translates to "liberated from thought." When you empty your mind though meditation, you are simply drowning out God's voice, since He forbids the practice.

The Biblical Concept of Meditation
There are many verses in the Bible that speak about meditation. The Biblical term "meditation" means to study or figure out the deepest meaning of a thing. It *never* means the emptying of the mind. Here are just a few verses that demonstrate this:

> "This book of the law shall not depart from your mouth, but you shall meditate on it day and night, so that you may be careful to do according to all that is written in it; for then you will make your way prosperous, and then you will have success."
> *Joshua 1:8*

"And I shall lift up my hands to Your commandments, which I love; and I will meditate on Your statutes." *Psalm 119:48*

"My eyes anticipate the night watches, that I may meditate on Your word." *Psalm 119:148*

Christians pray intelligently, not like the eastern pagans. For example, the Hindus repeat mantras, which are a word or phrase, over and over again.

Jesus especially commands us not to use the eastern pagan type of meditative prayer, but the true godly form of prayer.

"And when you are praying, do not use meaningless repetition as the Gentiles do, for they suppose that they will be heard for their many words." *Matthew 6:7*

I have had Wiccans tell me there is a difference between a prayer to a god or goddess and a meditative incantation or spell. A prayer is simply talking to a god or goddess and asking them for something. A spell requires an incantation and some meditative practice that puts you in an altered state of consciousness to enable you to pull power down and fix the problem yourself.

In conclusion
Christian prayer should be modeled after the Lord's Prayer, asking God for His blessing and guidance and thanking Him for all He has done. Prayer should not be confused with meditation. Christians should not be involved in any form of meditation or altered state of consciousness.

Ancient Paganism

Any church or Christian group that allows people to fall down and jerk, or go into uncontrollable shaking, is practicing sorcery. If they teach you must become unconscious to get healed or see visions, this is the same practice as sorcery.

Everything godly and of the Holy Spirit must be practiced in an orderly fashion as taught in 1 Corinthians 14.

> "Let all things be done decently and in order."
> *1 Corinthians 14:40*

Anyone who teaches you to replace normal intelligent prayer with an opening or emptying of the mind or any kind of eastern meditation, including breath prayers, walking a labyrinth, dynamic meditation, repeating words or phrases until you have an experience, is a practitioner of sorcery.

Any church that has statues (idols), images, or icons at prayer stations where you stare at them until you receive a vision is practicing a version of sorcery.

The Desert Fathers

(The last of the Gnostics)

Gnostics and the Desert Fathers

To open this chapter we need to define the people we will be studying.

The Ancient Church Fathers

The Ancient church fathers were the disciples of the twelve apostles and their immediate disciples. Their teachings were consistent until about the third century. Many books were written by the ancient church fathers, and still exist, that contrast the teachings of the apostles of Jesus Christ with the Gnostic cults of their day.

The Gnostics / Cults

During the first two centuries cults rose up that mixed the pure teaching of the Word of God with magic and sorcery. These groups were called Gnostics. Today Christians refer to groups who follow the Gnostic teachings as cults.

The Desert Fathers / Mystics

During the third century some occultic practices began to creep into the church. The first mystics or Christian occultists appeared during this time and are referred to as the "desert fathers."

Gnostic Paganism Tries to Conquer

The Church was so opposed to sorcery and magic that volumes of books were written on how and why the heretics were wrongly being guided by Satan. Both Irenaeus in the 170's AD and Hipolytus in the 220's AD wrote against these heresies.

According to the ancient church fathers, the Gnostic heresies started with Simon Magus about the year 32 AD.

Simon Magus

Simon was called a "magus." A magus is another term for magician or sorcerer. Luke wrote about him in the book of Acts.

> "But there was a certain man, called Simon, which beforetime in the same city used sorcery, and bewitched the people of Samaria, giving out that himself was some great one: To whom they all gave heed, from the least to the greatest, saying, This man is the great power of God. And to him they had regard, because that of long time he had bewitched them with sorceries."
> *Acts 8:9-11*

The Scripture teaches that this Simon did not repent of his sins and become a Christian; but instead saw the miracles that the apostles could perform and sought to buy this power from them with a large sum of money. This means he fully intended to continue to practice his sorcery and add to it, if possible, whatever it was that the apostles were doing. This would make him an even greater "god" in the minds of the people he deceived.

> "Now when Simon saw that the Spirit was bestowed through the laying on of the apostles' hands, he offered them money, saying, 'Give this authority to me as well, so that everyone on whom I lay my hands may receive the Holy Spirit.' But Peter said to him, 'May your silver perish with you, because you thought you could obtain the gift of God with money! You have no part or portion in this matter, for your heart is not right before God. Therefore repent of this wickedness of yours, and pray the Lord that, if possible, the intention of your heart may be forgiven you. For I

> see that you are in the gall of bitterness and in the bondage of iniquity.'" *Acts 8:18-23*

As we can see, the apostle Peter recognized through the power of the Holy Spirit that Simon had no intention of truly repenting. You can't be a Christian and practice sorcery. It is *not* possible!

Ancient church father Irenaeus described Simon Magus not only as the father of the Gnostic cults, but as a practitioner of sorcery by his use of magic and spirits in dreams.

> "Simon called Magus used exorcisms and incantations, love-potions, and charms, as well as those beings who are called 'Paredri' (familiars) and 'Oniropompi' (dream-senders)."
> *Irenaeus, Against Heresies 1.23*

Ancient church father Clement wrote that Simon left Israel prior to the ministry and crucifixion of Jesus Christ to study magic in Egypt (*Recognitions of Clement* 2.5-16). We will see that Egypt becomes a haven for the very last of the Gnostics and the center of their revival in 270 AD.

Alexander the Coppersmith
Paul said Alexander the coppersmith fell away from the faith.

> "Alexander the coppersmith did me much harm; the Lord will repay him according to his deeds. Be on guard against him yourself, for he vigorously opposed our teaching."
> *2 Timothy 4:14-15*

Tertullian, in his book *The Flesh of Christ 16*, recorded the details. Alexander developed a violent temper. He left the true faith and joined a subgroup of the Ebionites. This group taught that Jesus was just a man with a sin nature, there is no resurrection in the flesh, and humans can become sinless by obtaining the Christ consciousness.

The Spirit of Python

One other example of sorcery in the New testament is the girl who had the familiar spirit. She followed Paul around accurately speaking about things which she humanly could not have known about. Paul rebuked her; and knowing she was possessed of a demon, cast the demon out.

> "It happened that as we were going to the place of prayer, a slave-girl having a spirit of divination met us, who was bringing her masters much profit by fortune-telling. Following after Paul and us, she kept crying out, saying, 'These men are bond-servants of the Most High God, who are proclaiming to you the way of salvation.' She continued doing this for many days. But Paul was greatly annoyed, and turned and said to the spirit, 'I command you in the name of Jesus Christ to come out of her!' And it came out at that very moment. But when her masters saw that their hope of profit was gone, they seized Paul and Silas and dragged them into the market place before the authorities," *Acts 16:16-19*

This is an interesting story, not only because we are told she predicted the future through her demon-possession, but also because of the wording of the text. Where we have "spirit of divination" in our English translation, the Greek literally says "spirit of Python." This helps a lot, because those who predicted the future through the spirit of Python, called a pythoness, were those who served the Greek god Apollo as a Delphic Oracle. Many Greek texts describe the process how the Oracles entered an altered state of consciousness to make their predictions. In their case, most used drugs; but a few used only meditation. They stared at objects for so long they began to babble incoherently in their native language. Some began to speak in other archaic languages. Then petitioners could question them and they would make their predictions.

Notice the similarities. With the pythoness, whether through drugs or just mediation, the girl had to go through some process where she entered an altered state of consciousness.

Hymenaeus and Philetus
Hymenaeus and Philetus are mentioned in 2 Timothy 2:17. They were excommunicated because they began teaching that the Resurrection had already occurred. Paul writes about a very similar teaching in 2 Thessalonians 2:2, where heretics were teaching the Day of the Lord had already occurred. Both of these false doctrines are the basis of what we today call Preterism. (Preterism teaches that most, if not all, of the Biblical prophecies have already been fulfilled. In contrast, most Christians believe in premillennialism. Premillennialism teaches there are still many prophecies yet to be fulfilled.)

Phygelus & Hermogenes
Paul wrote in 2 Timothy that Phygelus and Hermogenes fell away from the faith.

> "You are aware of the fact that all who are in Asia turned away from me, among whom are Phygelus and Hermogenes." *2 Timothy 1:15*

Tertullian, in his book, *On the Resurrection*, said these two denied that there would be a resurrection of the physical body.

Tertullian also wrote in his book, *Prescription Against Heretics*, that Phygelus, Hermogenes, Philetus, and Hymenaeus were people who left the apostles and their true faith for a counterfeit. Tertullian concluded that this is what John was talking about when he said:

> "They went out from us, but they were not *really* of us; for if they had been of us, they would have remained with us; but *they went out*, so that it would be shown that they all are not of us."
> 1 John 2:19

This Gnostic sorcery continued into the second century. The second century fathers recorded Gnostic practices and severely denounced them.

Gnostic Sorcery

We will list only what the ancient church fathers recorded were Gnostic teachings and practices relating to sorcery. For a complete study on the Gnostic cults see the book *Ancient Prophecies Revealed* by the author.

Most Gnostics taught there was a goddess Sophia that sent the serpent into the Garden of Eden to free Eve and Adam. By eating of the tree, they attained true gnosis and were set free, by obtaining god/goddesshood.[15] Gnostics used mantras to effect nature.[10] (Similar teachings can be found in the Hindu mantra, Kabalistic letter magic, and the Kabalistic doctrine of emanations.)

Carpocratian Heresies
The Gnostic sect of Carpocratians was founded by Carpocrates, who was a magician and a fornicator.[40] Carpocratians taught the false doctrine that humans are imprisoned in a cycle of reincarnation by evil creator angels, but would eventually break the cycle and be saved.[8] They practiced magical arts, incantations, spells, and had voluptuous feasts. They were also in the habit of invoking the aid of subordinate demons and dream-senders.[49]

Heresies of Cerinthus
Cerinthus taught Jesus was just a man and "the Christ" descended on Him at His baptism and departed before He suffered on the cross. [12] (He taught the same heresy that Alexander the coppersmith taught. He taught Jesus was not the Christ, but there is a Christ consciousness we can all have.)

Heresies of Saturninus[7]
Saturninus taught that he, himself, was a creator angel.[7] He also believed that Jesus did not have a physical body,[7] and that the reason Jesus came to earth was to destroy the god of the Jews.[7] Saturninus taught that sex, marriage, and reproduction were sinful.[7,14] Saturninus and all who attended his school practiced vegetarianism and asceticism.[48]

Heresies of Menander
Menander taught that by means of magic, one may overcome the angels that made the world. [6]

Heresies of Marcion
Marcionites were strongly addicted to astrology,[29] and taught there would be no resurrection.[31] In his "gospel," Marcion removed references to Christ being the

Creator,[33] and taught Jesus was a phantom, having no physical body.[34]

Heresies of Alcibiades (Elchasai)

Alcibiades formed the Gnostic cult of the Elchasaites. Alcibiades taught there are female angels and a new remission of sins (based on the teachings of his book). Alcibiades' teachings were similar to the teachings of Callistus, that Christ was born merely a man. They used incantations, and believed in reincarnation and astrology.[52]

Heresies of Elchasaites

Some Elchasaites broke away and formed a subgroup that taught Jesus incarnated many times (Reincarnation). They used incantations and baptisms in their confession of elements (communion). They also involved themselves in astrological and mathematical science (Bible codes), and the arts of sorcery. They believed they had powers of prescience (precognition instead of a Word of Knowledge – a "self" power instead of a spiritual gift.)[53]

Heresies of Naasseni

The Naasseni worshiped the serpent and taught their order was started by James, the Lord's brother. They used the Gospel according to Thomas. They took some of their teachings from the Mysteries of Isis and some from the Mysteries of the Assyrians. They practiced orgies.[41]

Heresies of Basilides

Basilides taught reincarnation with karma.[25] Very much like shamans today, Basilides taught that spirits (human, animal, or other) can latch on to us and force us to sin.[23]

Heresies of Valentinus

Valentinus taught that saving faith comes from your spirit and that the Holy Spirit is really your human spirit. This false doctrine was revived by a modern cult called The Way International. They taught that only those whose spirit is an emanation from the goddess Sophia were predestined to be saved. All others were predestined to hell.[23]

"When they are called Phrygians, Novatians, Valentinians, Marcionites, Anthropians, or Arians they have ceased to be Christians."
Lactantius Divine Institutes 4.30

References

1. Irenaeus, Against Heresies 1.1-3
2. Irenaeus, Against Heresies 1.5
3. Irenaeus, Against Heresies 1.6
4. Irenaeus, Against Heresies 1.7; 4.37
5. Irenaeus, Against Heresies 1.21
6. Irenaeus, Against Heresies 1.23
7. Irenaeus, Against Heresies 1.24
8. Irenaeus, Against Heresies 1.25
9. Irenaeus, Against Heresies 1.7
10. Irenaeus, Against Heresies 1.14-15
11. Irenaeus, Against Heresies 1.13
12. Irenaeus, Against Heresies 1.26; 5.1
13. Irenaeus, Against Heresies 1.27
14. Irenaeus, Against Heresies 1.28
15. Irenaeus, Against Heresies 1.30
16. Irenaeus, Against Heresies 2.14
17. Irenaeus, Against Heresies 2.29
18. Irenaeus, Against Heresies 3.3
19. Irenaeus, Against Heresies 3.23
20. Titian, Greeks 13
21. Titian, Greeks 18
22. Clement of Alexandria, Instructor 2.2
23. Clement of Alexandria, Stromata 2.3,20; 4.13
24. Clement of Alexandria, Stromata 3.4
25. Clement of Alexandria, Stromata 4.12
26. Clement of Alexandria, Stromata 4.24
27. Clement of Alexandria, Against Heresies 4.29
28. Tertullian, Against Marcion 1.2
29. Tertullian, Against Marcion 1.18
30. Tertullian, Against Marcion 1.19-20
31. Tertullian, Against Marcion 1.24
32. Tertullian, Against Heresies 2.33
33. Tertullian, Marcion 2.17
34. Tertullian, Marcion 3.8, 4.8
35. Tertullian, Valentians 1.29
36. Tertullian, Valentians 1.30
37. Tertullian, Heresies 1.1
38. Tertullian, Heresies 1.2
39. Tertullian, Heresies 1.6
40. Tertullian, Treatise of the Soul 1.35
41. Hipolytus, Heresies 5.1
42. Hipolytus, Heresies 5.7
43. Hipolytus, Heresies 5.12
44. Hipolytus, Heresies 6.5-9
45. Hipolytus, Heresies 6.10
46. Hipolytus, Heresies 6.34-35
47. Hipolytus, Heresies 6.36-37
48. Hipolytus, Heresies 7.16
49. Hipolytus, Heresies 7.20
50. Hipolytus, Heresies 7.26
51. Hipolytus, Heresies 9.7
52. Hipolytus, Heresies 9.8-9
53. Hipolytus, Heresies 10.25

Master List of Gnostic Heresies

1. There is more than just one Christ
2. There is a Christ consciousness
3. There is no physical resurrection
4. Reincarnation

5. Karma
6. We are evolving into gods
7. You can develop psychic powers
8. Animals have spirits (shamanism)
9. The book of Genesis is not real history, but a myth

Evil Practices of Gnostic Heretics
10. Use of illicit, mind-altering drugs
11. Use of mantras and meditation in place of prayer
12. Use of sorcery
13. Orgies

By the mid 200's AD, Gnostic cults were all but stamped out in the western church. In Egypt, however, it was a different story.

Simon Magus in Egypt
We learned that ancient church father Clement stated that Simon Magus, the father of the Gnostics, left Israel prior to Jesus Christ's ministry and crucifixion. We are also told Simon left for the purpose of studying magic in Egypt. Clement does not say who Simon studied under or what he was taught specifically, but we have a pretty good idea.

Egyptian Essenes
Prior to the birth of our Lord Jesus, the Essenes in Israel studied the Scriptures while they lived secluded away from the common people. During this time there arose a different kind of Essene in Egypt. They, too, called themselves Essenes but differed from the Jewish Essenes in many ways. These Egyptians mixed many of the rites of magic and paganism into a Jewish context. Like most who deny the resurrection of the physical body, these Egyptian Essenes ended up believing in reincarnation and evolution.

Ancient Paganism

> "They abstained from wine, were vegetarians, were very ascetic, denied the bodily resurrection, kept the names of the angels (probably referring to 1 Enoch), learned the quality of roots and stones... they had their own special form of exorcism, had books on charms and magic, interpreted dreams... They had sunrise prayers (literally, prayers to or for the sun) in the same manner as the Therapeute."
> *Josephus Antiques 15.10.5 & 17.13.3; War 2.8.2,3,6*

Therapeute

The Therapeute were the first recorded "Christian" monastic sect. Shortly after Mark's arrival in Alexandria, Egypt, some of the Egyptian Essenes mixed strict Christian doctrine with their Jewish/pagan rites.

> "They took the concept of celibate orders of monks and nuns from the 'Vestal Virgins' from Greek and Roman pagan practices. They had sunrise prayers [literally, prayers to or for the sun] which may have been patterned after the [Egyptian] Essenes." *Eusebieus Ecclesiastical History 2.17*

Saint Anthony and the Desert Fathers

During the late first and early second century, Gnosticism gained much ground in the Christian world but was very close to being stamped out by the beginning of the third century, the 250's AD. In Egypt, however, there was no persecution of the Therapeute. In time the Egyptian Therapeute fragmented into more than twenty schools of monasticism. By the year 270, a man who will later be called Saint Anthony arrived in Egypt to study some of these practices. Until this time monastic meditative practices were still considered Gnostic sorcery by most of the western church.

The Catholic encyclopedia describes the desert fathers as the very first Christian monks. Officially these practices began under Saint Anthony in Egypt around 270 AD.

As you can see, we have historical proof that meditative practices, Christ / god consciousness, and the idea that everyone will be saved all come from the demonic world. They come directly from paganism, though the Gnostics and mystic Roman Catholics and into today's Emergent and New Age churches.

To the right is a list of famous mystics, ranging in time from 270 AD to the mid twentieth century. It is compiled from the book *Faith Undone*, by Roger Oakland, and the online Catholic encyclopedia, newadvent.org. We will learn just how highly the modern Emergent Movement respects Thomas Merton in a later chapter.

Name	Date AD
Saint Anthony	255-345
Palladius	368-431
Saint Benedict	480-543
Saint Gregory I	540-604
Bernard of Clairvaux	1090-1153
Francis of Assisi	1181-1226
Thomas Aquinas	1225-1274
Meister Eckhart	1260-1328
Thomas A Kempis	1380-1471
Ignatius DeLoyola	1491-1556
Teresa of Avila	1515-1582
John of the Cross	1542-1591
Thomas Merton	1915-1968

Summery from the ancient church fathers:
In contrast with this paganism, the disciples of the apostles taught that Christianity was completely different.

"The arts of astrologers, soothsayers, augurs, and magicians were made known by the angels who sinned, and are forbidden by God."
Tertullian Apology 35

"Christians do not employ incantations or spells to perform miracles." *Origen Against Celsus 1:6*

"Demons… invented astrology, soothsaying, divination, and those productions which are called oracles, necromancy, and the art of magic."
Lactantius Divine Institutes 2:16

"The Church does not perform anything by means of angelic invocations, incantations, or by any other wicked curious art; but, directing her prayers to the Lord." *Irenaeus Against Heresies 2.32*

"God is not to be sought after by means of letters, syllables, and numbers."
Irenaeus Against Heresies 2.25

"Astrology, soothsaying, divination, oracles, necromancy, and the art of magic are the invention of Demons and vain according to the Sybil. Magicians and Enchanters call demons by their true name and mingle false things with true."
Lactantius Divine Institutes 2.17

"As the days of Noah were,
so shall also the coming of
the Son of man be."

Matthew 24:37

The Coming of a New Age

Today, daytime television is full of New Age proponents. Sylvia Brown is frequently a guest on the Montel Williams show. Ms. Brown has formed her own church. She teaches there is no hell, no resurrection, and no salvation needed. She believes in reincarnation. Oprah Winfrey endorses many New Age teachers on her shows. Her guests include Neal David Walsh, Marianne Williamson, Rhonda Byrne and many others.

Oprah has publicly stated she is a Christian, but she is the kind of Christian that believes Jesus just came to give us the Christ consciousness. We have seen this is the very same belief the apostle Paul excommunicated the heretic Alexander for.

We have seen in previous chapters that we must believe and obey the teachings of Jesus Christ as presented in the Bible or we will die and go to hell.

> "Jesus saith unto him, I am the way, the truth, and the life: no man cometh unto the Father, but by me." *John 14:6*

Hindus, Buddhists, Wiccans, Kabalists, Sufis, Sheiks, and Muslims refuse to accept Jesus and His teachings. According to Jesus they are all headed to hell.

A New Age teaching denies there is a hell. It states there are many ways to God; God is in all of us (known as Lucifer's lie of emanation). And the practice of meditation will bring answers to all of our other questions.

We have learned Jesus told us specifically not to practice meditation like the heathen do. Basically, New Agers are calling Jesus Christ a liar.

Most New Agers are outside the church, or in other cases have been excommunicated by their denominations for heresy.

In the book *Ancient Prophecies Revealed*, we dedicated an entire chapter to the apostasy of the Church. The ancient church fathers listed 100 ways the church would fall into apostasy and become the harlot church as described in the book of Revelation.

About the end times, Jesus said many people would start thinking they are a "Christ" or have the Christ consciousness in themselves:

> "And many false prophets shall rise, and shall deceive many. For there shall arise false Christs, and false prophets, and shall show great signs and wonders; insomuch that, if it were possible, they shall deceive the very elect."
> *Matthew 24:11,24 NKJV*

False teachings and sorcery do not simply go away. Revelation shows us that during the time of the Antichrist and the seven-year Tribulation period, sorcery is at an all time high. Even though people suffer incredibly because of their practice of sorcery, they *refuse* to repent of it.

> "Neither repented they of their murders, nor of their sorceries, nor of their fornication, nor of their thefts." *Revelation 9:21*

Ancient Paganism

Even after the Second Coming of our Lord Jesus Christ, some people will still refuse to follow Him. Revelation states that outside the holy city will be those who *still* practice sorcery.

> "Outside are the dogs and the sorcerers and the immoral persons and the murderers and the idolaters, and everyone who loves and practices lying." *Revelation 22:15*

Oprah Winfrey

Talk show hostess Oprah Winfrey has said many times on her TV and radio shows that as she grew up she attended a Christian church. She still believes that she is a Christian. But during her early adulthood she read a book entitled *Discover The Power Within You*. This book was written by Unitarian minister, Eric Butterworth. It espouses the heresy that man is God.

James Redfield
Celestine Prophecy

Marianne Williamson
A Course in Miracles
A Return to Love

Neal David Walsh
Conversations with God
Friendship with God
The New Revelations

Rhonda Byrne
The Secret

Oprah wrote an endorsement on the front cover of the new edition of *Discover The Power Within You*, saying:

> "This book changed my perspective on life and religion. Eric Butterworth teaches that God isn't "up there." He exists inside each one of us, and it's up to us to seek the divine within."

Oprah has had many New Age heretics on her show. Unbeknownst to her viewers, many of her former Roman

140

Catholic and Protestant guests have been excommunicated from their former denominations for espousing these heresies.

On Youtube.com, many people have viewed the clips from Oprah's show where she states she believes God is within her, Jesus is not the only way to get to heaven, and Jesus only came to show us how to obtain the Christ consciousness.

Remember we discovered in an earlier chapter that the heretic Alexander taught the doctrine of a Christ consciousness. The Apostle Paul excommunicated Alexander from the church for this very teaching.

The Secret

Rhonda Byrne, author of The Secret, espouses the idea of a God/Christ consciousness, and that hell does not exist.

> "You are god in a physical body... You are all power... You are all inelegance... You are the creator." Rhonda Byrne, *The Secret*,

> "No matter who you thought you were, now you know the Truth of Who You Really Are. *You are the master of the universe.* You are the heir to the kingdom. You are the perfection of life. And now you know *The Secret.*"
> Rhonda Byrne, *The Secret*, p. 183

Neal David Walsh

Neal David Walsh claims God came to him and had him write his "Conversations with God." What Walsh's god told him completely contradicts what the God of the Bible tells us. One of them must be lying. According to the Bible, Walsh's god is no more than a demon.

Ancient Paganism

> "The twenty-first century will be a time of awakening, of meeting the creator within. Many beings will experience Oneness with God... There are many such people in the world now... These messengers and visionaries are heralds of the New Age."
> Neal David Walsh, *Friendship with God*, pp. 295-296

> "There is only one message that can change the course of human history forever, end the torture, and bring you back to God. That message is The New Gospel: WE ARE ALL ONE."
> Neal David Walsh, *Friendship with God*, p. 373

> "Yet let me make something clear. The era of the Single Savior is over. What is needed now is joint action, combined effort, collective co-creation."
> Neal David Walsh, *The New Revelations*, p. 157

> "You are already God, you simply don't know it."
> Neal David Walsh, *Conversations with God*, Book I, p. 202

> "You are One with everyone, and everything in the universe – including God."
> Neal David Walsh, *Tomorrow's God*, p. 311

Reiki

Reiki is the Japanese word for the occult "ghost energy." The term Reiki is now used as the title for an occultic, meditative type of massage therapy, similar to Therapeutic Touch, a form of meditation required for you to contact your Reiki spirit guides.

> "There are higher sources of help you can call on. Angels, beings of light and Reiki spirit guides..."
> William Lee Rand, *Developing Your Reiki Practice*

Yoga

Yoga is the Hindu word for "yoking" with Brahma. This Hindu god would be considered a demon by Christians. The way to yoke with this demon is by practicing a series of stretches and meditation.

Eckankar Mystics

Eckankar is a small cult that prides itself on practicing a version of astral projection they call "Soul Travel." I was able to attend a seminar they put on once in Olathe, Kansas. The main speaker talked about the superiority of their Soul Travel over standard astral projection. He also remarked that it was important to develop your psychic powers though meditation.

During the break I spoke with him and asked him a few questions. I mentioned that some studies I have read have found a link with meditation and mental illness. One example was a person with epilepsy. Studies show epileptics can have a seizure by staring at a blinking red light, while others could actually bring on a seizure by certain forms of meditation. He had heard of those studies and did not seem to want to dispute them.

This being the case, my question to him was:

> "If I begin to meditate, how do I know that what I am seeing is real or, possibly, a hallucination brought on by some short circuit I am causing in by brain? More importantly, how do I know can I be assured I will not damage myself by triggering some form of epileptic seizure?"

His answer surprised me. Instead of giving me a scientific reason for why I would be safe if I did it his way, he simply said:

"That's the risk every mystic takes."

Transcendental Meditation

I had a similar experience when I visited the center for TM studies in Kansas City. After speaking to the representatives there, they encouraged me to master the standard TM and then advance to the TM-Sidhi program where I would develop my psychic powers. The thing I noticed was both representatives seem to have been on drugs sometime in their lives. Both were very slow to think and answer, much like a normal human when first awakened from a deep sleep. My first though was why would someone trying to sell a product pick people who appeared to be damaged by drugs, to sell their product. My second thought was maybe it wasn't drugs that did that to them, maybe it was the meditation!

Beware of groups using New Age terms. These are a dead give away that something is wrong. Check for any of the following terms:

> Your higher self, higher consciousness, higher wisdom, ego, id, subconscious, super-conscious, higher plane, planetary transformation, paradigm shift, planetary conversion, global religion, global shift, centering, channeling, creative visualization, attuning, inner guidance, holistic health, human development, human potential, law of attraction, law of rebirth, mystery schools, mysticism, new thought, perennial wisdom, radiance technique, secret wisdom, self relaxation, transcendence, transpersonal, universal oneness, etc.

These terms refer to things that, in reality, do not exist. Stay away from people and groups that use terms like these. These are just confusion sent by Satan.

Word Faith Movement

Some New Age ideas have crept into the church with the Word Faith Movement. In its extreme form Word Faith taught the following:

1. We are becoming little gods because of Jesus' gift
2. We are developing the magic power of faith, whereby we can simply command God to do things for us or by our own faith power name things into existence.

Even though this was bad enough, they still taught orthodox Christian doctrine in that:

1. They did not meditate (practice sorcery)
2. They did not say God is in everyone and all faiths will lead to salvation.
3. They believed in the Resurrection, not reincarnation.
4. They taught Wiccans, New Agers, Buddhists, Hindus, and Muslims would die and go to hell because they rejected Jesus Christ.

In the twenty-first century we have seen the acceptance of the Word Faith heresy open wide a door for the Emergent movement to enter the church full force.

To hear audio clips of the Word Faith proponents teaching heresy, go to Biblefacts.org and select "Word Faith" under the cults section. There you will find a good number of MP3's of false teachings in their services.

Ancient Paganism

Some more popular Word Faith proponents:

John Bevere	Larry Huch
Morris Cerullo	T.D. Jakes, Bishop
Kim Clement	Joyce Meyer
Kenneth Copeland	Joel Osteen
Paul Crouch	Rod Parsley
Creflo Dollar	Peter Popoff
Jesse Duplantis	Fred Price
Kenneth Hagin (Rhema)	Oral Roberts
Marilyn Hickey	R.W. Shambach
Benny Hinn	Karl Strader
Rodney Howard-Browne	Robert Tilton

God In Your Midst

Many New Agers and some of the Word Faith proponents will misquote Jesus when he said the Kingdom of God is within you.

> "Neither shall they say, Lo here! or, lo there! for, behold, the kingdom of God is within you."
> *Luke 17:21*

The New American Standard Bible was a much clearer translation of this verse. From this translation, you can tell Jesus is telling the Pharisees not to look for another Messiah, because He is the Kingdom and is right there in their midst.

> "nor will they say, 'Look, here it is!' or, 'There it is!' For behold, the kingdom of God is in your midst." *Luke 17:21 NASB*

146

Druids and the labyrinth

Emergent Church

We have seen mysticism creep into the church from the pagans and Gnostic cults. We have documented that the ancient church was vehemently against the ideas of meditation, Christ consciousness, and man being divine. The ancient church fathers also prophesied that at the end of the church age many in the church would apostatize and adopt these false teachings.

We have traced the false doctrines that man is divine and the pantheistic idea that God is in everything, from the birth of the Mystics (Christian occultists) under Saint Anthony, c270 AD, up to Catholic Thomas Merton, c1968 AD.

Today we have a movement called the "Emergent Church" which is adopting these ideas of mediation, contemplative prayer, God/Christ consciousness, and universalism.

We will categorize these as "emergent mystics."

Emergent mystics are teaching:
1. There is a Christ consciousness
2. The Emergent Church can redefine and reshape Christianity in their own image
3. Biblical prophecy is not important
4. Mankind is divine (doctrine of emanations)
5. Occultic mediation renamed "contemplative prayer"
6. People of all faiths can be saved *without* Jesus Christ

Emergent Mystics and their *Books*

Bernard of Clairvaux
The Steps of Humility

Ignatius De Loyola
Spiritual Exercises

Thomas Merton
Conjectures of a Guilty Bystander

Matthew Fox
The Coming of the Cosmic Christ

Brian McLaren
The Church on the Other Side
A New Kind of Christian
Reinventing Your Church
A is for Abductive
A Generous Orthodoxy
The Secret Message Of Jesus

Dan Kimball
The Emerging Church
They Like Jesus but Not the Church

Henri Nouwen
Thomas Merton, Contemplative Critic
In the Name of Jesus
The Way of the Heart
Sabbatical Journey
Here and Now
Reaching Out

Doug Pagitt
Church Re-Imagined
Emergent Manifesto of Hope

Dallas Willard
The Spirit of the Disciplines

Jack Canfield
Key to Living the Law of Attraction

Rob Bell
Velvet Elvis
Sex God

M. Scott Peck
The Road Less Traveled

John Michael Talbot

Ken Blanchard

Donald Miller
Blue Light Jazz

Harry Emerson Fosdick
Modern Use of the Bible
Dear Mr. Brown

Brennan Manning
Abba's Child
All Above
Ragamuffin Gospel
The Signature of Jesus

Richard Foster
Celebration of Discipline
Devotional Classics
Spiritual Classics
Spiritual Formation
Be Still DVD
Renavore Bible

Erwin McManus
The Barbarian Way

Leonard Sweet
Quantum Spirituality
Soul Tsunami
Postmodern Pilgrims

Ancient Paganism

For a detailed study on these authors, the Emergent Movement, and their books, see the books: *A Time of Departing* and *For Many Shall Come in My Name* by Ray Yungen, *Faith Undone* by Roger Oakland, and *Deceived on Purpose* by Warren Smith.

Let's look at a few quotes to see just what the movement is teaching.

Emergent Religion
Emergents say religion is what we make of it. If it is not working, we must reinvent it. To work successfully, it must be a global one-world religion.

> "I foresee a resonance, 'a rebirth based on a spiritual initiative …This new birth will cut though all cultures and religions and indeed will draw forth the wisdom common to all vital mystical traditions in a global religious awakening I call 'deep Ecumenism,'"
> Matthew Fox, *The Coming of the Cosmic Christ, p. 5*

> "In the emerging culture darkness represents spirituality. We see this in Buddhist temples, as well as Catholic and Orthodox churches. Darkness communicates that something serious is happening."
> Dan Kimball, *The Emerging Church, p. 136*

> "The way of the cross, the way of Lao Tzu, the way of the Buddha, the way of Islam and the way of Judaism all speak of the same path… All refer to the same transformation of self."
> Marcus Borg, *The Heart of Christianity, p. 216*

This is what the Bible prophesies predict would be the state of the end time Apostate Church. But, then again. the Emergent Movement reinterprets prophecy, too.

Emergent Prophecy

End time prophecy is reinterpreted to be symbolic of who we overcome, by creating this one-world religion in which you can be saved *without* Jesus.

> "In the twinkling of an eye, we are all changed by this experience. It is a mass metanoia, a shared spiritual experience for the human race, a peaceful second coming of the divine in all of us as us."
> Barbra Marx Hubbard, *The Revelation*, p. 174

> "You are to prepare the way for the alternative to Armageddon, which is the Planetary Pentecost, the great Instant of Co-operation which can transform enough, en masse, to avoid the necessity of the seventh seal being broken."
> Barbra Marx Hubbard, *The Revelation*, p. 172

Emergent Jesus

Emergent proponents tell us we must forget about Jesus dying on the cross – it is too divisive. No one needs to believe in Jesus to be saved.

> "All human beings can walk though that [god's] door, whether they know Jesus or not."
> Henri Nouwen, *Sabbatical Journey, p. 149*

> "The church's fixation on the death of Jesus as the universal saving act must end, and the place of the cross must be reimagined in the Christian faith."
> Alan Jones, *Reimagining Christianity*, p. 132

Ancient Paganism

> "I don't believe that what we can know of Jesus is confined by the New Testament... There is no such thing as 'what really happened.'"
> Allen Jones, *Reimagining Christianity*, p. 209

What God has decided and prophesied will be and no amount of imagining will change that! To make the statement that all we have to do is re-imagine Christianity and reshape it into what we want it to be, is rebellion toward God. It is placing ourselves in God's place, which is blasphemy. It is exactly what the people at the Tower of Babel did. God said if He did not stop them, they would accomplish all they "imagined" to do.

The apostasy/emergent groups want us to re-imagine or reform Christianity. In Galatians, Paul said we are to seek the approval of God, not man. There is no need to reinvent Christianity. To even suggest such a thing is to admit Christianity, as we know it, is a lie.

In Genesis the serpent asked, "has God really said?" In other words, the old gospel is wrong and we need a new understanding. How could there be a new gospel every one hundred years? How could they all be true? Anyone who makes it up as he goes along has abandoned God!

If all of us are "god," if we will all be saved, and if there is no hell, then why does the Bible say *differently*? Why did God lie to us when the Bible was written? How can we believe *anything* this new god says?

> "For if someone comes to you and preaches a Jesus other than the Jesus we preached, or if you receive a different spirit from the one you received, or a different gospel from the one you accepted, you put up with it easily enough."
> *2 Corinthians 11:4 NIV*

Emergent Christ Consciousness

In the Emergent Church, we see the idea that God is in everyone and everything.

> "It is a glorious destiny to be a member of the human race... If only they could see themselves as they really are... I suppose the big problem would be that we would fall down and worship each other... At the center of our being is a point of nothingness which is untouched by sin and illusions, a point of pure truth... this little point... is the pure glory of God in us. It is in everybody."
> Thomas Merton, *Conjectures of a Guilty Bystander*, pp. 157-158

Emergent Contemplative Prayer

In Contemplative Prayer we see meditation replacing biblical prayer. As we learned in the chapter about the ancient Canaanites and Balaam, God considers this type of "meditation," sorcery.

> "Contemplative prayer is not so much the absence of thoughts as a detachment from them."
> Thomas Keating, *Open Mind, Open Heart, ch. 1*

> "Choose a biblical text with rich content for contemplation... Once you have "passed in" or "passed over" relinquish the words and enter into wordless prayer... Consider using a focal point for contemplative prayer. A painting of the face of Jesus may serve in this way..."
> Richard Foster, *Spiritual Classics*, p20

> "Listen to the mantra as you say it, gently but continuously... If thoughts of images come, these are distractions at the time of meditation, so return simply to saying your word. Simply ignore it and

the way to ignore it is to say your mantra. Return with fidelity to meditation each morning and evening for between twenty and thirty minutes."
Paul T. Harris, *Silent Teaching: The Life of Dom John Main*, pp. 320-332

"Many Christians use 'Breath Prayers' throughout their day. You choose a brief sentence, or a simple phrase that can be repeated to Jesus in one breath."
Rick Warren, *The Purpose Driven Life*, pp. 89, 299

"Buddha points to the path and invites us to begin our journey to enlightenment. I... invite you to begin your journey to enlightened work."
Ken Blanchard, *What Would Buddha Do at Work*, Forward

"Beyond these models of reconciliation, a theology of mysticism provides some hope for common ground between Christianity and Islam."
Tony Campolo, *Speaking My Mind*, p. 149

"Walking the Labyrinth" is a form of dynamic meditation. Dynamic meditation is when you do the same thing over and over again until it empties the mind in much the same way a mantra does.

"The experience of walking the labyrinth invites the body into a rhythm of moving around and moving toward the center, then back out."
Doug Pagitt, *Church Re-Imagined, p. 103*

The Bible tells us "not to be ignorant of Satan's devices." Do we really need Wiccan and Druidic rituals and devices to get closer to God? Or is it drawing us closer to Lucifer?

Dangers of Meditation

In the chapter on Prayer vs. Meditation, I told you of my experiences with the Eckankar Mystics, and how everyone there knew of the dangers of meditation.

It has been reported that those who practice Contemplative Prayer often experience the same serious problems as the Hindus when practicing the serpent meditation commonly referred to as Kundalini Meditation.

Emergent Church speaker, Richard Foster, warns other emergents of the same dangers inherent with contemplative prayer in his book.

> "I want to give you a word of precaution. In the silent contemplation of God we are entering deeply into the spiritual realm... *sometimes it is not the realm of God* [emphasis mine] even though it is supernatural... there are various orders of spiritual beings, and some of them are definitely not in cooperation with God and His way! ...A prayer of protection should be said beforehand, something to the effect of 'all dark and evil spirits must now leave'"
> Richard Foster, *Prayer: Finding the Hearts True Home*, p. 157

> "Contemplative prayer is not for the novice. I do not say this about any other form of prayer... Contemplation is different. While we are all equally precious in the eyes of God, we are not equally ready to listen to 'God's speech in his ...all embracing silence.'"
> Richard Foster, *Prayer: Finding the Heart's True Home*, p. 156

Ancient Paganism

Why would a Christian put himself or herself in a position of demonic attack when they could simply pray the way Jesus commands and not have to worry about it?

Prayer Stations with Icons

Ancient church father Hypolytus wrote about what became of the seventy disciples that Jesus sent out two by two. He wrote that Demas forsook the faith and became a priest of idols. My guess is that he became a priest of the Carpocratians. They were the first of the Gnostics to use idols of Jesus and the saints. This was heavily condemned by the ancient church.

Clement of Alexandria in *Stromata 3:431*, and Tertullian in *Against Ebion 3*, mention the Carpocratian Gnostic sect committed a unique kind of sin in that they used small idols of Jesus, Aristotle, Pythagoras, other people, and angels, which they said were a means to contact the pure God. They would adorn the idols with wreaths, garlands, and in other ways honor them. Today many Christians see nothing wrong with honoring statues of saints or praying to them. About proper and improper prayer, the ancient church fathers said:

> "The Church does not perform anything by means of angelic invocations, or incantations, or by any other wicked curious art; but, directing her prayers to the Lord." *Irenaeus Against Heresies 2.32*

> "Mature Christians pray only to God, without thought for bodily position or set time (eg. In a meditative setting) and their prayers are not selfish." *Clement of Alexandria, Stromata book 7.7*

The apostle John says:

> "Little children, guard yourselves from idols."
> *1 John 5:21*

The apostle Paul goes a step further and says an obedient Christian will not even *associate* with a Christian who has anything to do with idols.

> "But actually, I wrote to you not to associate with any so-called brother if he is an immoral person, or covetous, or an idolater, or a reviler, or a drunkard, or a swindler--not even to eat with such a one."
> *1 Corinthians 5:11*

In a vision, the prophet Ezekiel saw the priests in the Jerusalem Temple worshiping in ways forbidden by God. God punished them for setting up prayer stations with icons (mainly Egyptian) on the walls. In doing this they were admitting everything represented God and meditative sorcery was acceptable.

When a person enters a Catholic, Orthodox, or Protestant Church to stare at an image to achieve an altered state of consciousness in order to experience a vision, this amounts to idolatry and sorcery. Being demonically seduced into believing you are god also amounts to idolatry.

Prophecy – How to Prove What Is Right
Do not trust your mystical experiences since you can't predict future events; rather, trust the Old Testament prophets who have proven they were in contact with the one true God by the prophecy they left behind. Their prophecy has proven itself to be 100% accurate. We must judge all things by what the Bible says.

The Bible records hundreds of prophecies Jesus fulfilled while He was here on earth. During that first one hundred years of the Church Age, thirty-five prophecies were fulfilled. During the 1,816 years Israel was out of the Holy Land, only twenty-three prophecies were fulfilled. Since Israel was reestablished as a nation in 1948 AD, there have been fifty-three prophecies fulfilled in stunning detail. All of these, plus the next fifteen unfulfilled prophecies, are given in chronological order in the book *Ancient Prophecies Revealed,* by the author.

So you see, Christianity can't evolve or change. The prophecies are set in stone!

We learned in the chapter entitled Occult Tools that occult tools like tarot cards and astrological charts do not work in and of themselves. They only stand a chance of working if a form of meditation / alternate state of consciousness is achieved. The same thing holds true inside the church: relics, holy water, crucifixes, statues of saints and angels, prayer stations and labyrinths can't really do anything by themselves, either. For any of these things to begin to work, it takes an altered state of consciousness. But...

Sorcery is forbidden!

The Jerusalem Temple

Future Antichrist Religion

In this book you've learned that Lucifer wants humans to think we are becoming gods. He wants us to meditate, which the Bible describes as sorcery. He wants us to believe there many ways to be "saved," and that you don't need either Jesus Christ or repentance, because there is no hell to worry about.

In the future when the Antichrist steps on the scene of human history, he will say the same things.

The apostle Paul describes the Antichrist actually sitting in a rebuilt Jewish Temple, in Jerusalem, Israel. When he takes his seat in the Temple, he will make the announcement to the world that he is God incarnate. He will also insist that he is more God that any god previously worshiped on earth, including Jesus.

> "...that man of sin be revealed, the son of perdition; Who opposeth and exalteth himself above all that is called God, or that is worshipped; so that he as God sitteth in the temple of God, shewing himself that he is God."
> *2 Thessalonians 2:3-4*

This is Lucifer's lie: that the Antichrist is an emanation of what once was the original creator God.

The prophet Daniel describes the religion of the Antichrist in this way:

> "And the king shall do according to his will; and he shall exalt himself, and magnify himself above every god, and shall speak marvellous things against the God of gods, and shall prosper till the

indignation be accomplished: for that that is determined shall be done. Neither shall he regard the God of his fathers, nor the desire of women, nor regard any god: for he shall magnify himself above all. But in his estate shall he honour the God of forces: and a god whom his fathers knew not shall he honour with gold, and silver, and with precious stones, and pleasant things."
Daniel 11:36-38

There are over eighty prophecies in the Bible about the Antichrist and the Tribulation period. For a detailed study of all of these, see the book *Ancient Prophecies Revealed.*

The Antichrist will not worship or give any regard to any of the gods we know of that are worshiped on earth today. He will not regard Jesus Christ, Buddha, Allah, Krishna, or any of the ancient gods worshiped long ago.

Instead he will worship a "god of forces." As demonstrated in this book, this god is not a personal, intelligent, loving god, but simply the energy in each one of its creation and the left-over energy from what it once was.

The Antichrist will claim to be the highest evolved being, and demonstrate this by what the Bible calls lying signs and wonders.

"Even him, whose coming is after the working of Satan with all power and signs and lying wonders," *2 Thessalonians 2:9*

The religion and method of the Antichrist's deception will be based on the ancient Babylonian mystery religion. We have seen this is a delusion caused by meditative sorcery.

Ancient Paganism

> "...for by thy sorceries were all nations deceived. And in her was found the blood of prophets, and of saints, and of all that were slain upon the earth." *Revelation 18:23-24*

Most people will follow the Antichrist and take his mark. Even those who are warned will refuse to repent of their sorcery.

> "Neither repented they of their murders, nor of their sorceries, nor of their fornication, nor of their thefts." *Revelation 9:21*

The prophet Isaiah warns us:

> "And when they shall say unto you, Seek unto them that have familiar spirits, and unto wizards that peep, and that mutter: should not a people seek unto their God? for the living to the dead? To the law and to the testimony: if they speak not according to this word, *it is* because *there is* no light in them." *Isaiah 8:19-20*

The apostle Paul warns us wizards, people with familiar spirits and the like are all connected to the devil and not to God.

> "But *I say*, that the things which the Gentiles sacrifice, they sacrifice to devils, and not to God: and I would not that ye should have fellowship with devils." *1 Corinthians 10:20*

The statement that a loving God would not send anyone to hell is a doctrine of demons.

Conclusion of the Matter

You must understand Lucifer wants you in hell! He has designed a very convincing plan to get you there. Stay away from anything that is connected to mindless meditation, and the occult. You are not a god and you will never become a god. You can, however, spend eternity with God, who loves you very much and does not want you to spend eternity in hell.

We are all sinners and have fallen short of the grace of God. Every one of us is destined for hell. God loved us so much that He sent His son, Jesus, to pay for our sins by dying on the cross and fulfilling the ancient prophecies.

All you have to do is recognize that you are a sinner and need the free gift of eternal life. Accept Jesus as your personal Lord and savior. Begin studying the Bible and get into a Bible-teaching church.

Please contact us at Biblefacts.org if you have questions or if we can help you find a good Bible- teaching church.

Appendices

Source Documents

In an effort to bring out the most accurate information on the most ancient form of paganism, we looked for all the information we could get from ancient Jewish history books, as well as comments from the ancient church fathers.

Jewish History Books		
Name	**Date**	**Comments**
Genesis	1450 BC	Completely Accurate – Word of God Has accurate dates
Jasher	1400 BC	Highly accurate history book Has accurate dates
Josephus	70 AD	Useful information Has inaccurate dates
Jubilees	100 BC?	Contains some useful information Has inaccurate dates and information
Mishna	200 AD	Compiled oral traditions Is mostly accurate
Talmud	400-800 AD	Commentary on the Mishna Has some inaccurate information, and mostly accurate dates until 587 BC

Genesis
We used the Book of Genesis, which is the divinely inspired Word of God, and is 100% accurate in every way.

Jasher
The book of Jasher is a highly accurate history book that has the recommendation of Scripture. See Joshua 10:13; 2 Samuel 1:18; and 2 Timothy 3:8. The *Ancient Book of Jasher* is available thought Biblefacts Ministries, biblefacts.org.

Josephus

Josephus used the Greek version of the Scriptures, so his information is good, but his dates are way off.

Jubilees

The book of Jubilees uses a calendar that mixes the lunar and solar calendars for its dates. As of yet no one has accurately deciphered how the jubilee calendar works. The book itself has many stories that contradict Scripture; so we must only use its information when it can be verified by other sources.

Mishna

The Mishna is the Jewish oral law (all the details for sacrificing animals, for instance.) We assume it is mostly accurate.

Talmud

The Talmud is accurate in its dates until the destruction of the first Temple in 587 BC. Since it is commentary on the Mishna, it does contain inaccurate information and speculation.

Other Books By Ken Johnson, Th.D.

Ancient Post-Flood History
Historical Documents That Point to Biblical Creation.

This book is a Christian timeline of ancient post-Flood history based on Bible chronology, the early church fathers, and ancient Jewish and secular history. This can be used as a companion guide in the study of Creation science. This revised edition adds the background history of nine new countries. Learn the true origins of the countries and people of France, Germany, Denmark, Sweden, Ireland, Scotland, Greece, Italy, Russia, Egypt, Israel, Iraq, Iran, China, the Arabs, the Kurds, and more.

Some questions answered: Who were the Pharaohs in the times of Joseph and Moses? When did the famine of Joseph occur? What Egyptian documents mention these? When did the Exodus take place? When did the kings of Egypt start being called "Pharaoh" and why? Who was the first king of a united Italy? Who was Zeus and where was he buried? Where did Shem and Ham rule and where were they buried? How large was Nimrod's invasion force that set up the Babylonian Empire, and when did this invasion occur? What is Nimrod's name in Persian documents? How can we use this information to witness to unbelievers?

Ancient Seder Olam
A Christian Translation of the 2000-year-old Scroll

This 2000-year-old scroll reveals the chronology from Creation through Cyrus' decree that freed the Jews in 536 BC. The *Ancient Seder Olam* uses biblical prophecy to prove its calculations of the timeline. We have used this technique to continue the timeline all the way to the reestablishment of the nation of Israel in AD 1948.

Using the Bible and rabbinical tradition, this book shows that the ancient Jews awaited King Messiah to fulfill the prophecy spoken of in Daniel, Chapter 9. The Seder answers many questions about the chronology of the books of Kings and Chronicles. It talks about the coming of Elijah, King Messiah's reign, and the battle of Gog and Magog.

This scroll and the Jasher scroll are the two main sources used in Ken's first book, *Ancient Post-Flood History*.

Ancient Prophecies Revealed
500 Prophecies Listed In Order Of When They Were Fulfilled

This book details over 500 biblical prophecies in chronological order; these include pre-flood times though the First Coming of Jesus and into the Middle Ages. The heart of this book is the fifty-three prophecies fulfilled between 1948 and 2008. The last fifteen prophecies between 2008 and the Tribulation are also given. All these are documented and interpreted from the Ancient Church Fathers.

The Ancient Church Fathers, including disciples of the twelve apostles, were firmly premillennial, pretribulational, and very pro-Israel.

Ancient Book of Jasher
Referenced in Joshua 10:13; 2 Samuel 1:18; 2 Timothy 3:8

There are thirteen ancient history books mentioned and recommended by the Bible. The Ancient Book of Jasher is the only one of the thirteen that still exists. It is referenced in Joshua 10:13; 2 Samuel 1:18; and 2 Timothy 3:8. This volume contains the entire ninety-one chapters plus a detailed analysis of the supposed discrepancies, cross-referenced historical accounts, and detailed charts for ease of use. As with any history book, there are typographical errors in the text but with three consecutive timelines running though the histories, it is very easy to arrive at the exact dates of recorded events. It is not surprising that this ancient document confirms the Scripture and the chronology given in the Hebrew version of the Old Testament, once and for all settling the chronology differences between the Hebrew Old Testament and the Greek Septuagint. The Ancient book of Jasher is brought to you by Biblefacts Ministries, Biblefacts.org

Third Corinthians
Ancient Gnostics and the End of the World

This little known, 2000-year old Greek manuscript was used in the first two centuries to combat Gnostic cults. Whether or not it is an authentic copy of the original epistle written by the apostle Paul, it gives an incredible look into the cults that will arise in the Last Days. It contains a prophecy that the same heresies that pervaded the first century church would return before the Second Coming of the Messiah.

The Rapture
The Pretribulational Rapture of the Church Viewed From the Bible and the Ancient Church

This book presents the doctrine of the pretribulational Rapture of the church. Many prophecies are explored with Biblical passages and terms explained.

Evidence is presented that proves the first century church believed the End Times would begin with the return of Israel to her ancient homeland, followed by the Tribulation and the Second Coming. More than fifty prophecies have been fulfilled since Israel became a state.

Evidence is also given that several ancient rabbis and at least four ancient church fathers taught a pretribulational Rapture. This book also gives many of the answers to the arguments midtribulationists and posttribulationists use. It is our hope this book will be an indispensable guide for debating the doctrine of the Rapture.

The Ancient Church Fathers
What the Disciples of the Apostles Taught

This book reveals who the disciples of the twelve apostles were and what they taught, from their own writings. It documents the same doctrine was faithfully transmitted to their descendants in the first few centuries and where, when, and by whom, the doctrines began to change. The ancient church fathers make it very easy to know for sure what the complete teachings of Jesus and the twelve apostles were.

You will learn, from their own writings, that the first century disciples taught on the various doctrines that divide our church today. You will learn what was discussed at the seven general councils and why. You will learn who were the cults and cult leaders that began to change doctrine and spread their heresy and how that became to be the standard teaching in the medieval church. A partial list of doctrines discussed in this book are:

Abortion	Free will	Psychology
Animals sacrifices	Gnostic cults	Reincarnation
Antichrist	Homosexuality	Replacement
Arminianism	Idolatry	theology
Bible or tradition	Islam	Roman
Calvinism	Israel's return	Catholicism
Circumcision	Jewish food laws	The Sabbath
Deity of Jesus	Mary's virginity	Salvation
Christ	Mary's assumption	Schism of Nepos
Demons	Meditation	Sin / Salvation
Euthanasia	The Nicolaitans	The soul
Evolution	Paganism	Spiritual gifts
False gospels	Predestination	Transubstantiation
False prophets	premillennialism	Yoga
Foreknowledge	Purgatory	Women in ministry

For more information visit us at:

Biblefacts.org

Bibliography

1. Cruse, C. F., *Eusebius' Ecclesiastical History*, Hendrickson Publishers, 1998.
2. Eerdmans Publishing, *Ante-Nicene Fathers*, Eerdmans Publishing, 1886.
3. Keating, Geoffrey, *The History of Ireland (BOOK I-II),* London, Irish Texts Society, 1902.
4. Hodges, Richmond, *Cory's Ancient Fragments*, London, Reeves and Turner, 1876.
5. Whiston, William, *The Works of Flavius Josephus*, London, Miller & Sowerby, 1987. Includes Antiquies of the Jews.
6. Pezron, Paul, *The Antiquities of Nations*, Mr. D. Jones, translator (London: R. Janeway, publisher, 1706.
7. Ken Johnson, *Ancient Post-flood History*, Xulon Press, 2006
8. Ken Johnson, *Ancient Seder Olam*, Xulon Press, 2007
9. Louis Ginzberg, *The Legends of the Jews*, Johns Hopkins University Press, 1948.
10. Ken Johnson, *Ancient Book of Jasher*, Createspace, 2008
11. Karel van der Toorn, *Dictionary of Deities and Demons in the Bible*, Brill, 1999
12. Ray Yungen, *A Time of Departing*, Lighthouse Trails, 2006
13. Roger Oakland, *Faith Undone*, Lighthouse Trails, 2007
14. Ken Johnson, *Third Corinthians*, Createspace, 2008
15. Ken Johnson, *Ancient Prophecies Revealed*, Createspace, 2008
16. Warren Smith, *Deceived On Purpose*, Mountain Stream Press, 2004
17. Ray Yungen, *Many Shall Come In My Name*, Lighthouse Trails, 2007

Printed in Poland
by Amazon Fulfillment
Poland Sp. z o.o., Wrocław

34270481R00098